THE

Responsive Advisory Meeting Book

150+ Purposeful Plans for Middle School

FROM RESPONSIVE CLASSROOM®

with Michelle Benson • Rio Clemente • Nicole Doner

Jeannie Holenko • Dana Januszka • Amber Searles

All net proceeds from the sale of this book support the work of Center for Responsive Schools, Inc., a not-for-profit educational organization and the developer of the *Responsive Classroom*® approach to teaching.

© 2018 by Center for Responsive Schools, Inc.

ISBN: 978-1-892989-90-1
Library of Congress Control Number: 2017954631

Photographs by Jeff Woodward
Illustrations by Lynn Zimmerman, Lucky Dog Design

Center for Responsive Schools, Inc.
85 Avenue A, P.O. Box 718
Turners Falls, MA 01376-0718

800-360-6332
www.responsiveclassroom.org

Contents

Responsive Advisory Meeting Overview

Responsive Advisory Meeting bolsters students' academic and social-emotional growth and provides meaningful opportunities to build positive relationships with peers and adults at school.

What Is Advisory?

An Advisory program is a critical component of middle school because it connects a teacher (the advisor) with a group of students (the advisees) to provide academic and social-emotional support and to strengthen the community of the school. The primary objectives of a structured, purposeful Advisory program are to:

➡ Support students in building positive, meaningful relationships with one or more caring adults at school

➡ Help students develop positive relationships with their peers

➡ Provide a safe place for students to strengthen their academic and social-emotional competencies, explore their interests more deeply, and nurture the development of new skills and talents

Responsive Advisory Meeting, which is a key *Responsive Classroom* middle school practice, has a set, predictable structure. Each meeting is organized around one of seven distinct purposes that underlies the meeting's topic and activities. Responsive Advisory Meeting thus offers a solid framework for building meaningful connections and developing respectful and trusting relationships, while meeting students' developmental needs to belong, feel significant, and have fun. Responsive Advisory Meeting:

➧ Empowers students to create relevant connections to the school at large and with students who share similar interests (sports teams, clubs, and so on)

➧ Strengthens the community of learners by providing opportunities for positive student-student and student-teacher interactions

➧ Improves academic performance by helping students develop an academic mindset

➧ Communicates about the life of the school

The Responsive Advisory Meeting plans in this book are based on comprehensive research conducted by Center for Responsive Schools at seven public middle schools (rural, suburban, and urban). Over 250 middle school students in grades six, seven, and eight generated ideas and tested them in teacher-led student focus groups and Advisories. For more information on this research, see the "Research and Development on Responsive Advisory Meeting Purpose Topics" report at www.responsiveclassroom.org/printables.

The Benefits of Responsive Advisory Meeting

Responsive Advisory Meeting benefits students in a variety of significant ways.

Promotes a sense of community

By providing a safe space to develop respectful, trusting relationships, such as by sharing multiple perspectives on various topics, Responsive Advisory Meeting helps to create and extend connections among all members of the Advisory community. Each component is designed to incorporate positive social interactions, helping students to be known and to get to know others.

Meets students' needs for belonging, significance, and fun

Social science theory and research by Maslow, Dreikurs, Adler, and others confirm that once basic needs are met (food, water, shelter, etc.), all human behavior is motivated by the need for:

Belonging—the feeling of knowing you are a part of something greater than yourself. Examples: Students feel a sense of belonging when they know how to function (because expectations have been taught) and are recognized as a contributing member of a learning community. Students feel like they are a part of a community when classmates express concern after their absence.

Significance—being known for a strength, talent, or characteristic. Examples: Students feel a sense of significance when they are able to use their talents (such as to create a poster for the room) or when they are known among friends for a skill (such as giving good advice).

Fun—finding joy in a situation, being engaged, and feeling motivated. Examples: Students feel joyfully engaged when they are appropriately challenged during a whole-group activity, when sharing a piece of knowledge about their interests, or when laughing together during Advisory.

Responsive Advisory Meeting is designed to meet these needs as students engage with their peers in purposeful, structured activities.

Improves students' academic performance

Responsive Advisory Meeting helps students develop and strengthen skills and build an academic mindset (that they belong in this school; that their effort improves performance; that they feel they can succeed academically; that they see the value in their work). Students have opportunities to explore and grapple with engaging, challenging content, collaborate with one another, build perseverance, and learn how to set and reach goals.

Encourages communication

Throughout Responsive Advisory Meeting, students can strengthen key listening, speaking, and other communication skills that are needed for success in and out of school when they communicate about their personal and academic lives. Responsive Advisory Meeting also provides an outlet for schoolwide communication.

Builds essential social-emotional learning (SEL) skills

Responsive Advisory Meeting is designed to help students build SEL competencies in cooperation, assertiveness, responsibility, empathy, and self-control. These SEL competencies are essential for academic success, for healthy relationships, and for job readiness.

The Power of Responsive Advisory Meeting: The Four Components

The purpose-driven format of Responsive Advisory Meeting enables students to experience the full power of Advisory and enables schools to meet all the objectives of a strong Advisory program.

Ideally, Responsive Advisory Meeting takes place at a regular time each day (or most days) for about 20 minutes. This length of time allows students to move through all four Responsive Advisory Meeting components and have meaningful conversations and interactions with their peers and advisor.

In schools that don't yet have a devoted time for Advisory or that have limited time scheduled, teachers can adapt Responsive Advisory Meeting to use during a few minutes of homeroom time or before class. Even with a shortened Advisory, students will still experience many of its benefits.

Each of the four components of Responsive Advisory Meeting plays an integral part in achieving the overall goals of Advisory, and taken together, they are a powerful combination. The four components are:

Arrival welcome—The advisor welcomes each student by name as they enter the classroom.

Announcements—In advance, the advisor writes an interactive message and displays it where it can be easily seen and read by all students.

Acknowledgments—In pairs or small groups, students share their responses to a prompt in the announcements message, a piece of news about themselves, or ideas about a topic related to their studies or interests.

Activity—The whole group does a fun, lively activity that's focused on the specific purpose of the meeting.

Each meeting concludes with a question or statement that prompts student reflection on the meeting's purpose.

Each of these four components plays an essential role in creating positive energy, engagement, and feelings of mutual respect and belonging.

Arrival welcome

The advisor stands at the door to welcome students individually and greet them by name as they enter the room. It's important to make eye contact (as long as the student is comfortable with that) and to use a friendly voice and neutral body language. The purposes of the arrival welcome are to:

➡ Set a positive tone

➡ Provide a sense of welcome and recognition

➡ Create a space in which students feel emotionally safe

➡ Communicate respect

You can add variety to your arrival welcome by greeting students in a language other than English (ask native speakers for help with pronunciation or search online) or by adding a welcoming gesture, such as a handshake, micro-wave (wave a pinky), high five or high ten, or fist bump.

Announcements

The announcements component provides information in the form of a written message that relates to the academic curriculum or social aspects of classroom life. Each announcements message focuses primarily on one topic that ties into the meeting's purpose, with content that is relevant to all students. It should be posted where all students can easily read it as they walk into the room and get settled—for example, on an easel or a whiteboard. The purposes of the announcements message are to:

➡ Prompt thinking and encourage students to take positive actions, individually and as a group

➡ Connect students with one another and the greater school community

➡ Promote effective school-to-student communication (such as upcoming classroom activities and team or schoolwide events)

The announcements message has four parts:

Salutation—Many advisors use a letter-style salutation, such as "Dear Seventh Graders" or "Good Morning, Problem-Solvers!" Whatever the choice of words, the greeting is friendly in tone and tells students "This message was especially written for you—come and read it!"

Sample Announcements Message

Welcome, Progress Makers!

We're nearing the end of the first quarter. This is an excellent time to review your SMART goal plan and evaluate your progress. If you've already reached your goal, congrats! Now's a great time to set some new goals.

Get your SMART goal sheets. On a sticky note, write down your distractors—things that get in the way of making progress toward your goals. Be ready to share.

Notes and Events

- ✓ Our monthly all-school meeting is this Friday.
- ✓ Mrs. Cruzan is starting a robotics club. Beginners are welcome. Want to join? Leave a note in the "Robotics" basket on her desk.
- ✓ Don't forget to ask your parent/guardian to sign your permission slips for after-school activities. Slips are due this Wednesday.

Body—The message body offers a few brief statements about the day's topic. An inspirational quote can be added for variety.

Prompt—This invites students to interact in some way with the message and is related to the purpose of the meeting. The prompt may be a simple activity to complete or a question or statement that stimulates thinking.

Notes and events—The message concludes with a brief list of upcoming dates students need to be aware of, extracurricular opportunities, or required actions students need to take.

As you compose your messages to the class, consider students' interests and developmental needs, and what is happening in their classrooms, school, and wider community. Students may benefit from being explicitly taught specific procedures of reading and interacting with the announcements message. Interactive Modeling (see page 13) is an effective practice for teaching procedures such as:

- Asking a classmate or advisor for clarification
- Using the response method to a prompt (sticky note, index card, partner chat)

➡ Getting settled quietly while other classmates are interacting with the message

The announcements message gains its power from the student-student and student-advisor interactions it generates as students read the message and respond to the prompt.

Acknowledgments

Students greet each other by name and share their responses to the announcements prompt or a question or topic you pose. This sharing may be personal or academic, based on the Advisory purpose. Since acknowledgments topics often spring from their direct experience, students are motivated to engage in the conversations. The purposes of acknowledgments are to:

➡ Give students multiple opportunities to make personal connections and get to know each other better

➡ Help students build essential communication and social-emotional skills

➡ Reinforce content and academic skills

➡ Strengthen the classroom community

Students may share with a partner, a small group, or both, and there may also be opportunities to share a summary or idea with the whole group. To get the most out of both the greeting and the sharing part of acknowledgments, students need a variety of communication skills. Interactive Modeling (see page 13) is an effective practice for teaching many of these skills, such as:

➡ Choosing school-appropriate topics to talk about

➡ Stating a main idea with supporting details

➡ Asking friendly questions to elicit more information

Here are some ways to support students as they learn to exchange news, ideas, and opinions.

Give clear directions—Setting clear parameters in your directions can help students stay on topic. For example, instead of saying "Tell me about your engineering project," narrow the focus by saying "Share one important aspect of your engineering project."

Use sentence stems (or starters)—Posting a sentence stem on an anchor chart for students to complete will help them focus and also reinforce their use of complete sentences.

For sixth graders, a sentence stem might be: "My favorite character in our book is _____ because _____."

For eighth graders, a sentence stem might be: "I want my self-portrait to convey these three key ideas about myself: _____, _____, and _____."

Use think-alouds—To model how to decide on one idea among many to talk about, you might do a think-aloud to narrate your thought process. If the topic is "Kinds of problems I like to solve," your think-aloud could sound like this: "Hmm. I really like math problems, but these aren't the only kind of problems I like to solve. Trying to set up our own soccer game after school can cause problems, like how to choose teams and which team goes first. I like to solve that kind of problem, too, so that's what I'll talk about."

Brainstorm ideas—When you first introduce acknowledgments, ask students to brainstorm possible ways to acknowledge and respond appropriately to the speaker. To give students some ideas to draw on, write their ideas on a chart before doing acknowledgments.

Prepare students to handle serious news—Emphasize that students should always bring serious news (such as a traumatic event in their neighborhood) to you first. Sometimes, you'll need to help a student modify the serious news to make it school-appropriate; at other times, you may need to explain that certain information is not suitable for sharing with the group.

Responding to serious news requires skills that even many well-intentioned adults have not mastered; we still struggle to find the right words to offer. Let middle schoolers generate ideas for constructive responses to serious news. You might ask, for example, "If someone shares something sad, what can you say to let them know that you really heard what they said and care how they feel?" By practicing responses to serious news during acknowledgments, students will feel more competent at navigating these situations now and as they grow into adulthood. (See page 198 for an example of a Responsive Advisory Meeting plan that you can use for dealing with serious news and difficult events.)

Activity

Responsive Advisory Meeting activities are brief, lively, and interactive, and they involve the whole group. They help build a positive community while supporting crucial learning goals. Some activities provide extra practice with key academic skills, such as comparing characters' responses to challenges they face or practicing deductive reasoning. Other activities offer practice in important social-emotional skills, such as listening and responding to the speaker and asserting one's opinions positively and respectfully. The purposes of the activity are to:

- ➡ Focus on the meeting's purpose

- ➡ Foster active and engaged participation that promotes cooperation

- ➡ Reinforce a sense of belonging and community

- ➡ Strengthen academic and social-emotional skills

It's important to teach students key skills to help make the activity component a success. Interactive Modeling (see page 13) is an effective practice for teaching a variety of self-control and cooperation skills, such as:

- ➡ Taking turns and making sure everyone is included

- ➡ Assisting classmates if they need help

- ➡ Handling mistakes respectfully

Here are some more ways to support students in being successful with these whole-group activities.

Choose activities that fit the group at the time—Group activities vary widely, although all involve movement of some kind. Some are playful, while others are more serious; many draw or expand on the curriculum; some are brainteasers, and some tap students' artistic side. When choosing activities, consider maturity levels, academic and social-emotional skill levels, and group dynamics. Early in the year, you may want to choose simpler activities that help students get to know each other, such as Four Corners (see page 37) or Just Like Me (see page 34). Later in the year, when students are more comfortable with each other and a level of trust has been built, turn to more complex or curriculum-based activities, such as Role-Play (see page 171) or Tag Team Graffiti (see page 133).

Look to academics for activity ideas—Think about the curriculum, and talk with cross-discipline colleagues on your team to find out what students are studying or need support with. For example, early in the year, you may want to focus some activities on content review and skills practice. As students become more confident in their abilities and with each other, you can increase the complexity of the academic content and/or skills in the activity. Remember also that students will be more likely to take academic risks that promote learning when activities are engaging and done in the spirit of collaboration.

For information about activity ideas that keep students engaged, check out *Middle School Motivators! 22 Interactive Learning Structures* and *Refocus and Recharge: 50 Brain Breaks for Middle Schoolers* (both published by Center for Responsive Schools, 2016).

Getting Started With Responsive Advisory Meeting

To learn, students must take risks, and students are typically more willing to take risks when they trust that they will be respected and valued. Responsive Advisory Meeting helps create that climate of trust. Everyone starts and ends the meeting together, being welcomed and welcoming each other, sharing news, listening to individual voices, and communicating as a caring group. This makes a powerful statement: every person counts. To plan an effective Responsive Advisory Meeting:

Choose a purpose

Each Responsive Advisory Meeting has a specific purpose that underlies the plan's topic and activities. On the Monday of a heavy testing week, students may benefit from a plan that supports academic readiness to refresh their test-taking skills and boost their confidence. On Wednesday, as testing continues, students might benefit from a plan that gives them a mental break and helps them recharge.

The following is an explanation of each purpose, along with a description of the advisor's roles and responsibilities, which change depending on the purpose.

 Build student-to-student affiliation—Middle school students are in a period of significant developmental changes. As their need for autonomy increases, they learn to navigate new school experiences and seek new peer connections. Meetings based on this purpose enable students to get to know one another on a deeper level and build stronger, more positive relationships.

Advisor's role: To support students as they develop relationships with their peers.

 Support academic readiness—Every middle school has a set of academic goals for its students. Meetings based on this purpose help students achieve academic goals through a "whole child" lens. While the focus is on helping students meet the achievement standards, consideration is also given to helping them develop the academic and social-emotional skills that are essential for positive academic performance.

Advisor's role: To ensure that students get varied, targeted, and engaging learning activities that are curriculum-based; to help students develop a set of skills that enable them to engage in rigorous academics.

Strengthen advisor-advisee relationships—For middle school students to be successful, it's critical that they have a positive mentoring relationship with at least one adult at school who knows and cares about them. As students get to know and trust one another during their Advisory time together, it's also important that they get to know and trust their advisor. Meetings based on this purpose center around topics and activities that help deepen personal connections between advisors and students.

Advisor's role: To develop relationships with a group of students and interact with them in ways that build trust; to get to know each student personally and serve as a mentor and advocate.

 Develop communication and social skills—Sometimes there's an expectation that middle school students should already have well-developed communication and social skills. In reality, these skills need to be explicitly taught to all students, every year. Meetings with this purpose focus on helping students develop skills such as listening attentively, speaking effectively, and demonstrating cooperation, assertiveness, responsibility, empathy, and self-control. These skills enable students to interact with others in prosocial ways and develop positive relationships.

Advisor's role: To teach these skills directly, provide time for practice, and have students set and monitor goals for developing these skills.

 Energize and re-engage—After sustained periods of academic focus, middle school students can benefit from engaging activities that involve movement. The goal of this purpose is to give students a brief mental break and recharge them for the learning ahead.

Advisor's role: To effectively manage activities that are fun, physically active, and energizing while helping students develop positive social-emotional skills.

 Reflect and recalibrate—Since school is a significant part of students' lives, there may be times when the primary purpose of Advisory is to think and talk about events that are happening in school. Meetings can include topics such as taking care of school property, preparing for high school, or taking actions against bullying. Other critical issues—such as conflicts in the school or greater community that may have caused harm—may also be addressed.

Advisor's role: To provide leadership, clarity, and support as students discuss important issues; to help students reflect on and invest in doing their part to create a vibrant, healthy school community where they can flourish.

Extend learning through themes—During the middle school years, students hone their talents and often develop lifelong hobbies, interests, and skills. Theme-based Advisories may cross grade levels and be organized into groups of students with similar interests. They often extend to service learning projects and may include partnerships with businesses and other organizations in the community. Meetings with this purpose also provide an opportunity for older students to mentor younger students.

Advisor's role: To provide meaningful opportunities for students to learn through exploration, develop their talents, and make strong connections with others who share similar interests; to help students become increasingly independent and competent in their areas of interest.

Set the tone

Because a teacher's language—words, tone, and pace—is one of the most powerful tools available, speaking positively to students during Advisory helps ensure their success. Effective teacher language conveys faith in students' abilities and intentions, and focuses on their actions rather than their character or personality. Here are some types of teacher language that support students' success in Advisory (and in all areas of school).

Reinforcing language identifies and affirms students' positive actions and accomplishments, encouraging them to continue to learn and grow: "You backed up your ideas with evidence."

Reminding language prompts students to remember for themselves the expectations you taught: "What's one thing you can do if your group gets stuck on a challenge?"

Open-ended questions draw on middle schoolers' thoughts, knowledge, skills, experiences, and feelings, and acknowledge their eagerness to share their ideas: "What do you already know about [empathy; test-taking skills; community service]?"

For more information on teacher language, see *The Power of Our Words for Middle School: Teacher Language That Helps Students Learn* (Center for Responsive Schools, 2016).

Establish ground rules and procedures

It's important to establish some ground rules and procedures that will help Responsive Advisory Meeting run smoothly. These rules and procedures can be advisor-generated or created collaboratively with the group and might be different from your classroom or team rules. Often, advisors include ground rules stating that all students are expected to participate, to be respectful of other ideas and opinions, and to be active listeners. With both advisor-created and co-created rules, it's important to discuss, teach, and model expectations over the first few weeks of Responsive Advisory Meeting. It's also helpful to post an anchor chart of these expectations where students can easily reference them.

Teach routines and signals

Each component of Responsive Advisory Meeting has its own routines—how to greet someone respectfully, how to actively listen to and share information, how to move safely during an activity, and how to work cooperatively. Think about which routines and signals you'll need to teach and model for your Advisory students. For example:

→ What should greeting you, the advisor, at the door look and sound like?

→ What do students need to do when they enter the room and read the announcements message?

→ How should students interact with each other when doing acknowledgments at their tables?

→ What signals will students need to know and respond to during activities (for example, a signal for quiet attention or a signal for starting and stopping)?

Interactive Modeling is an effective practice for teaching any classroom routine, including those used in Responsive Advisory Meeting. Interactive Modeling eliminates the confusion that often results from the assumption that if students are simply told how to do something, they'll "get it." Rather than telling, Interactive Modeling shows students exactly how a procedure looks and sounds, and allows them to practice. The built-in steps of modeling, noticing, and reinforcing are a powerful combination that enables students to engage with their learning of a new routine, behavior, or skill more deeply and with greater clarity. The four steps are:

1. Describe what you will model and why.

2. Model while students notice.

3. Give students the opportunity to collaborate and practice.

4. Reinforce their practice with immediate feedback.

For more information on Interactive Modeling, see *Interactive Modeling: A Powerful Technique for Teaching Children* by Margaret Berry Wilson (Center for Responsive schools, 2012).

The Power of the Circle

Throughout history and across cultures, people have come together in a circle to build, enhance, and celebrate community. Whether telling stories around a fire or performing a sacred ritual, gathering together in a circle taps into our sense of connection and shared humanity—and bringing students together in a circle during Advisory can do the same.

While sitting or standing in a circle, students can see one another, which helps them actively listen to and respond to one another and build a sense of community and belonging. In addition, this format encourages participation and makes it easier for the advisor to gauge students' understanding and adjust instruction or conversation topics accordingly.

The circle environment is also an ideal space for addressing conflicts or other difficult situations in a way that allows everyone to feel like equals—everyone sitting or standing together, the same distance apart, without hierarchy. During Advisory, you can use a circle to help students:

Get to know each other—Especially at the beginning of the year, it's essential to build a respectful and supportive Advisory community that's conducive to getting along and getting work done. The circle provides a space for students to share information about themselves, connect with others, and form a sense of shared identity.

Prepare for learning—The circle is a great space to introduce new or upcoming Advisory topics and build excitement about them. When students know the purpose behind what they're learning, they feel more invested. Introducing topics

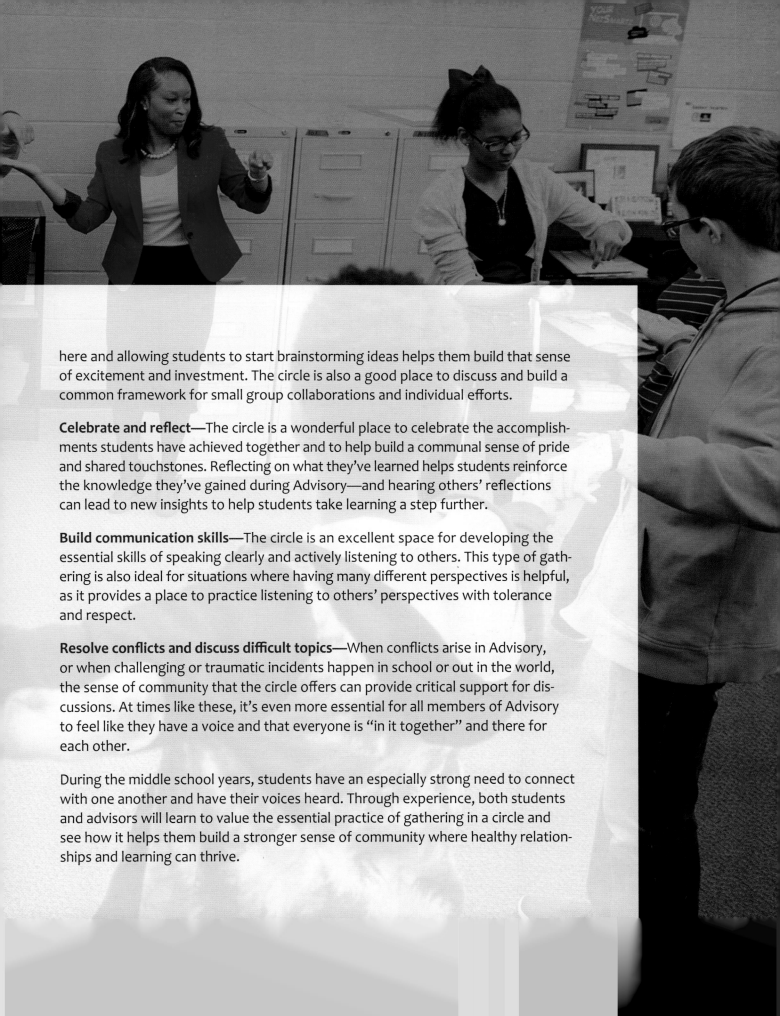

here and allowing students to start brainstorming ideas helps them build that sense of excitement and investment. The circle is also a good place to discuss and build a common framework for small group collaborations and individual efforts.

Celebrate and reflect—The circle is a wonderful place to celebrate the accomplishments students have achieved together and to help build a communal sense of pride and shared touchstones. Reflecting on what they've learned helps students reinforce the knowledge they've gained during Advisory—and hearing others' reflections can lead to new insights to help students take learning a step further.

Build communication skills—The circle is an excellent space for developing the essential skills of speaking clearly and actively listening to others. This type of gathering is also ideal for situations where having many different perspectives is helpful, as it provides a place to practice listening to others' perspectives with tolerance and respect.

Resolve conflicts and discuss difficult topics—When conflicts arise in Advisory, or when challenging or traumatic incidents happen in school or out in the world, the sense of community that the circle offers can provide critical support for discussions. At times like these, it's even more essential for all members of Advisory to feel like they have a voice and that everyone is "in it together" and there for each other.

During the middle school years, students have an especially strong need to connect with one another and have their voices heard. Through experience, both students and advisors will learn to value the essential practice of gathering in a circle and see how it helps them build a stronger sense of community where healthy relationships and learning can thrive.

Helpful Hints for a Successful Responsive Advisory Meeting

Responsive Advisory Meeting uses a predictable structure that helps to create clear expectations and a sense of security and trust. This purposeful meeting structure sets the tone for respectful engagement as it builds and enhances interpersonal connections. Students quickly recognize and understand the components of the Responsive Advisory Meeting, so they become grounded in its structure and are better able to engage cooperatively in meaningful exchanges. Here are some tips to help ensure your success with Responsive Advisory Meeting.

Know your students

Knowing students as individuals is essential to teaching them well. Adolescence is a time of tremendous physical, cognitive, and social-emotional change. At the beginning of each purpose's section in this book, you'll find tips that highlight typical developmental milestones for each grade. Keep these tips in mind as you plan and implement your Responsive Advisory Meeting and adjust activities to best meet the developmental needs of your students.

Plan purposefully

Be aware of the changes in your school. For example, during the first week or so of the school year, you might plan meetings that build student-to-student affiliation. At the end of the quarter, you might plan meetings that focus on students' reflection on their academic and personal challenges and achievements.

Form pairs and small groups thoughtfully

Think about the purpose of the meeting and the learning goal, as well as students' abilities and interests, when assigning pairs or groups. Some ways to form groups are mixed abilities, mixed interests, similar abilities, similar interests, or randomly. When you think students are ready to be respectful and inclusive, give them some autonomy in choosing their own partners or groupmates.

Start simple and build to more complex meetings

When the school year begins, students will need time to get to know each other and build their comfort level with their peers. When choosing acknowledgments and activities early in the school year, focus on topics and activities that aren't too personal or challenging. As the year progresses, scaffold or adapt activities to the needs of your Advisory community. As time passes, students will be more comfortable and ready to take on more academic and social-emotional risks.

Adapt meetings to fit your needs and your schedule

Each Responsive Advisory Meeting plan has ideas for each component. You can use these ideas as written, adapt them to meet the needs of the students in your Advisory, or use them as a springboard for creating your own ideas.

The ideal length of a Responsive Advisory Meeting is twenty minutes, which allows enough time for students to move through all components and have meaningful conversations and interactions without going beyond the threshold of students' attention spans. However, if your school does not have a dedicated time for Advisory, Responsive Advisory Meeting can be adapted to fit where your schedule allows it, such as during homeroom or before class, to ensure that there are opportunities for students to experience regular Advisory meetings.

Communicate with parents

Ongoing communication with parents will help them see Responsive Advisory Meeting for the vital learning time that it is. You can connect with parents in person or by letter, email, or phone. At the beginning of the year, introduce Responsive Advisory Meeting and its components and purposes. Explain the benefits of Advisory and its primary objectives to strengthen student-advisor and student-student relationships while helping students further develop their academic and social-emotional learning skills. You can access a sample letter to parents explaining Advisory at www.responsiveclassroom.org/printables.

Throughout the year, be sure to send Responsive Advisory Meeting updates. You may also want to let parents know ahead of time when your Advisory group will be discussing difficult topics or sharing serious news during acknowledgments. Reassure them that you'll always carefully monitor the information that students want to share.

Binder Checks During Advisory

Doing binder checks purposefully can help promote responsibility, independence, and academic readiness. To help students use their time efficiently when organizing a binder, do a quick Interactive Modeling lesson on how to organize one. You may also want to provide students with a list of what should be in their binder.

Communicate with colleagues and staff

At the beginning of the year, you might want to meet with the other teachers on your team, and with other staff and administrators, about using Responsive Advisory Meeting. For example, teachers on your team could review the plans in this book together to create a schedule for the first quarter or semester that everyone on the team can use, thus providing the entire team of students with a more consistent Advisory experience. (See pages 26–27 for a week-by-week sample schedule of plans that supports the ebb and flow of a typical school year.)

You could also brainstorm ideas for adapting the plans in this book or for creating your own plans and implementing them with the entire team of students. In addition, various aspects of Responsive Advisory Meeting, such as welcoming each student as they enter the classroom and providing more opportunities for students to work together, can also be adapted for use during classroom periods and even woven into lesson plans. (See pages 200–207 for five-minute plans designed for use during classroom periods.)

Consider inviting other teachers, staff, and administrators to participate in one or more of your Responsive Advisory Meetings. Many of the plans in this book offer activities that benefit (and sometimes involve) the greater school community. Some plans, such as the ones in the Interviewing School Leaders Advisory week (see pages 118–121), include communicating or planning with other teachers, staff, and administrators. You'll want to be sure to inform them ahead of time about their possible involvement to help these plans run smoothly.

Making the Most of This Book

The best way to get started using Responsive Advisory Meeting is to dive right in. Check out:

Plans-at-a-glance by purpose charts to choose plans that suit your specific purpose (see pages 22–25)

Week-by-week sample schedule of plans to implement Responsive Advisory Meeting plans for a 36-week period, showing one way the plans in this book can be used over the course of a full school year (see pages 26–27)

Tips at the beginning of each purpose's section for tailoring your meetings to meet students' developmental needs

One-day plans for specific occasions, such as when leaving on a long holiday break or returning from one (see pages 188–199)

Five-minute plans for days when regular Advisory isn't scheduled and for schools that have limited time for Advisory (see pages 200–207)

The more students participate in Responsive Advisory Meeting, the more they'll discover that Advisory is a safe, supportive community where everyone is welcomed, heard, and appreciated. During their time together in Advisory, students will discover that they can accomplish more than they expected through hard work and make important, enduring connections. As a result, they'll feel a stronger sense of community with their peers, with you as their advisor, and with the school as a whole.

Responsive Advisory Meeting sets a positive tone for the entire school by helping students develop respectful, trusting relationships, build confidence in their learning abilities, and meet their needs for belonging, significance, and fun.

Visit us online to download sample materials and handouts

Some plans (where noted) include sample cards, handouts, or other materials you can download and print to help you prepare and for students to use during Responsive Advisory Meeting. You can find the complete list at www.responsiveclassroom.org/printables.

Responsive Advisory Meeting Plans-at-a-Glance

The charts on the following pages will help you schedule your Responsive Advisory Meeting plans to suit your specific Advisory needs.

The plans in this book are organized by purpose and can be used at any point during the school year. Each four-day set of plans focuses on a theme and can be used over the course of the week or spread out over several weeks. You may also want to mix and match individual days, addressing two or more purposes in a week.

This book also includes one-day plans that address specific occasions and five-minute plans that can be incorporated into any class. A number of factors, such as testing dates, the school calendar, and students' developmental needs, can help guide you in choosing plans.

To find a plan that suits a particular purpose, check out the Plans-at-a-Glance by Purpose charts on pages 22–25. Or, check out the Plans-at-a-Glance Week-by-Week on pages 26–27 for one way to plan meetings for a quarter, a semester, or an entire school year.

Plans-at-a-Glance **by Purpose**

Build Student-to-Student Affiliation

THEME	DESCRIPTION	PAGE
First Impressions	Make personal connections to Advisory group and learn Advisory routines	32
Life Stories	Strengthen the Advisory community by sharing personal interests and learning about others	36
All About Respect	Brainstorm and discuss what respect looks like in the school setting	40
Inspiring Others	Examine how teamwork and positive actions promote individual and group success	44
End-of-Year Celebration	Look back on the year in Advisory and look forward to next year	48
Peer Pressure Role-Play	One-Day Plan	192
Making Connections	Five-Minute Plan	203

Support Academic Readiness

THEME	DESCRIPTION	PAGE
Goal for Gold	Set academic goals and create concrete plans to achieve them	54
Effort Equals Success	Learn how effort, persistence, and personal responsibility lead to academic success	58
Goals Revisited	Practice debate skills, and brainstorm ways to overcome distractions in pursuit of goals	62
Setting New Goals	Set new goals or revise old ones, and incorporate new habits for reaching them	66
Rebooting Study Skills	Plan new strategies and academic behaviors for tackling tests and assignments	70
Goals, Take 3	Visualize new goals; identify personal strengths and stressors in pursuit of new goals	74
Goals Wrap-Up	Map out a plan for reaching year-end goals	78
After a Long Break	One-Day Plan	193
Exploring a Concept	Five-Minute Plan	204
Introducing a New Unit	Five-Minute Plan	205

Strengthen Advisor-Advisee Relationships

THEME	DESCRIPTION	PAGE
Admiration Nation	Form a stronger Advisory community through the sharing of values and discovery of commonalities	84
Building Trust	Become personally invested in building trust through brainstorming, reflection, and creative activities	88
Student-Led Advisory Planning	Practice organization and cooperation by planning an Advisory meeting (with coaching by advisor)	92
Student-Led Advisory Week	Exercise leadership and independence by running an Advisory meeting	96
Whole-Team Meeting	One-Day Plan	194

Develop Communication and Social Skills

THEME	DESCRIPTION	PAGE
The Art of Communication	Discover how kindness and respect lead to more meaningful communication	102
Speaking Up	Experience how engaged, compassionate communication strengthens community bonds	106
Difficult Situations	Discuss and practice strategies for resolving challenging social situations	110
Walk the Talk	Clarify which qualities lead to success, and share through group presentation	114
Interviewing School Leaders	Interview members of school staff to learn qualities of an effective leader	118
What's the Outcome?	One-Day Plan	195
Practicing Observation Skills	Five-Minute Plan	206

Energize and Re-engage

THEME	DESCRIPTION	PAGE
Life Stories, Take 2	Strengthen the Advisory community by learning about multiple perspectives and sharing interests	124
Strengthening Self-Control	Devise strategies for, and experience the impact of, slowing down and thinking before speaking or acting	128
Motivation 2.0	Brainstorm how to stay motivated and identify people who can help with this goal	132
Finishing the Year Strong	Reflect on academic achievements and personal growth to pinpoint strategies that lead to success	136
Before a Long Break	One-Day Plan	196
Celebrations	One-Day Plan	197

Reflect and Recalibrate

THEME	DESCRIPTION	PAGE
Empathy	Explore how empathy can be put into action to create a safer school environment	142
Prioritize and De-stress	Develop strategies to de-stress and balance social and academic expectations with personal priorities	146
A Fresh Start	Brainstorm ways to overcome obstacles and stay motivated to begin a new semester or quarter with focus and intention	150
Reflecting and Envisioning	Reflect on recently met goals and Advisory experiences to identify skills that can help with future achievements	154
Teamwork and Team Spirit	Reflect on independent leadership projects to plan for future successes	158
Traumatic Events	One-Day Plans	198

Extend Learning Through Themes

THEME	DESCRIPTION	PAGE
Our Common Interests	Foster community by planning activities based on common interests	164
Safety For One and All	Gain a better understanding of the importance of safety and learn how to support safety for all in school	168
Handling Stress	Identify stressors, and outline plans for managing them	172
Community Outreach	Strengthen community through the planning of a community service project	176
Honoring Diversity	Understand others' perspectives and experience how diversity strengthens communities	180
Upstanding Students	Devise and practice plans to prevent bullying in school to build a safer community	184
Friendship Calculator	One-Day Plan	199
Pros and Cons	Five-Minute Plan	207

Plans-at-a-Glance Week-By-Week

1st Quarter

2nd Quarter

Build Student-to-Student Affiliation

Support Academic Readiness

Strengthen Advisor-Advisee Relationships

Develop Communication and Social Skills

Energize and Re-engage

Reflect and Recalibrate

Extend Learning Through Themes

3rd Quarter

4th Quarter

A Closer Look

For ease of use,
each meeting plan
is set up in a clear,
consistent format,
as shown at right.

Color-coded purposes

Goals for the week

Goal for Gold

Set academic goals and create concrete plans to achieve them

Skills Practiced This Week

Goal-setting
Responsibility
Self-motivation
Teamwork
Time management

List of skills practiced

Tips for success

TIP Tell students that the key to reaching a goal is creating a plan to support it. Explain that they will begin creating that plan today by turning their goal into a SMART goal: Specific, Measurable, Achievable, Relevant, and Time-Bound.

DAY 1 ■ Setting Goals

Arrival Welcome

Greet each student by name as they enter. Remind students to read the announcements message.

Announcements

Welcome, Goal Setters!

This week you're going to set goals for the 1st semester and create an action plan to achieve them.

A Goal Story, Part 1 At age 8, Michael had a goal: "I would like to make the Olympics." Years later, when he was a teenager, Michael made the team. You'll learn more about Michael tomorrow.

Think about a goal you'd like to achieve in a class over the next 3 weeks. Be ready to share.

Include upcoming school and team events in your messages this week.

Acknowledgments

Partner Chat At tables, students greet each other by name. Then they partner up to share their response to the announcements prompt. If time allows, students share their partner's goal with their table group.

Activity

Creating a SMART Goal [them in writing their goa] [to get a B on the next m] [again.]

Reflection "How does se [I pass my math test'?"

*A SMART goal template is a[

Activity directions

54 The Responsive Classroom Advisory Book

DAY 2 ■ Planning How to Reach a Goal

Guided Brainstorming Directions

◆ Each table group defines "effort" in their own words and shares the definition with the whole group. Facilitate reaching a whole-group consensus definition of "effort."

◆ With the consensus definition as a guide, students record four efforts that will help them progress toward their goal. For example: "If my goal is a B on the math test, one effort I can make is to study math for 15 more minutes each night."

◆ Each table group discusses how effort relates to change and shares their ideas with the whole group. Find commonalities among ideas, and emphasize the connection between effort and change.

◆ Students record four small changes that are likely to result if they put in their four efforts. For example: "If I study math for 15 more minutes each night, I expect to understand the chapter content better."

Arrival Welcome

Greet each student by name as they enter.

Announcements

Hello, Action Planners!

Today we're going to create a plan of action so you can reach your SMART goal. There are two parts to this plan: Effort and Small Changes.

A Goal Story, Part 2 Through thousands of hours of practice, Michael made four more Olympic teams and ended up winning the most Olympic medals in history. Maybe you remember him—Michael Phelps.

Get your SMART goal sheet from yesterday and review it. Sit with your table group and chat about the connection between effort and change.

Point out today's key school and team events.

Acknowledgments

What's the News? In their table group, one student begins by greeting the student to their left by saying "Good morning, _____. What's the news?" The student greeted responds with "Good morning, _____. The news is I have set a goal to [student shares goal from their SMART goal sheet]." Continue around the table until all students have been greeted and have shared their goal.

Activity

Creating a SMART Goal Plan Students stay in their table groups and use their SMART goal sheet from Day 1. Through guided brainstorming (see directions in margin), they explore this question together: "How does effort lead to change?" Then they complete the middle two columns on their SMART goal sheet. Collect the SMART goal sheets to use again.

Reflection Ask students to share with their table group one "aha" moment they had about effort leading to change while creating their SMART goal plan.

Build Student-
to-Student Affiliation

4-Day Plans

Tips for Building Student-to-Student Affiliation

All Grades

Early on in Advisory, students are in search of meaningful relationships and have a strong need to be with their friends. Reminding students to greet each other by name each day will not only help to build a positive learning community but also address students' need to get to know others and be known by others.

As the school year progresses, be mindful of the beginning of cliques. Remember to regularly mix students up in different pairings and groupings. Pay attention to the dynamics within these groups and provide guidance (or change the groups) as needed.

The final weeks of school, like any transitional period, will be full of mixed feelings and perspectives. Mindfulness activities will help students stay centered as they reflect back on the year and look ahead.

Grade Six

Sixth graders may be anxious and struggling to acclimate to the middle school setting. Emphasize getting to know each other, learning collaboratively, and being kind to each other.

Sports and outdoor activities are typically very important for this age group. They'll often argue about the rules and compare themselves to others. Guide students in participating in healthy activities, being good teammates, and working on improving their own skills versus being "the best."

This age group may show behaviors like eye rolling and a "whatever" posture if they feel uncomfortable or threatened. Saving face is important: If a conflict arises, give students time and space to calm down and reflect. Silliness, restlessness, and limit testing are all expected, so be sure to be empathetic and keep a light attitude while students are working to keep it together.

Grade Seven

Because seventh graders want to have meaningful relationships with peers and adults, provide opportunities for students to talk with each other and various adults in school. Emphasize the importance of speaking and listening with respect.

With their growing capacity for self-awareness, empathy, and abstract thinking, this age group can benefit from exploring challenging topics in depth. Give them opportunities to share their ideas in a safe environment.

Students in this age group have lots of physical energy and tend to need lots of sleep, food, and exercise. Providing snack breaks and brain breaks can help rejuvenate them physically and mentally. Their high energy also supports their taking on more leadership responsibilities, which can help bridge their transition to more adult roles in school and the community.

Grade Eight

Eighth graders expect to be noticed by adults, seen as important and capable, and accepted by their peers—and can be sensitive and defensive if they feel that they aren't. Because of this sensitivity, many students prefer solitary activities or working in pairs, so they'll benefit from extra support when working in groups.

There can be vast physical and emotional differences between boys and girls at this age, but both view hygiene and appearance as very important. Acknowledge eighth graders' strong feelings of insecurity, stress, or anxiety. Emphasize positive peer pressure, acceptance of oneself and others, and healthy balancing of time demands.

For many eighth graders, this marks the start of their transition to high school—a new building with new social and academic challenges. Focus on growth and accomplishment to help build their confidence.

First Impressions

Make personal connections to Advisory group and learn Advisory routines

---

Skills Practiced This Week

Active listening
Building community
Cooperation
Empathy
Making connections

DAY 1 ■ Welcome to Advisory!

Arrival Welcome

Greet each student by name as they enter. Teach and model how students should read and interact with the announcements message (see page 13).

Announcements

> Welcome to Advisory!
>
> Our Advisory program is a key way that adults at school can support students in building positive relationships and having a successful year.
>
> What do you think is the most important quality for getting along with others? For example, do you think it's being a good listener? Be prepared to share your ideas with a partner.

Include upcoming school and team events in your messages this week.

Acknowledgments

Partner Chat Pair students up with someone at their table group. After greeting their partner by name, they take turns sharing their responses to the announcements prompt. Then partners introduce each other to their table group. Model the introduction: "This is Maya. Maya thinks having empathy for other people is the most important quality for getting along with others." Circulate and listen in on each group; note some responses.

Activity

Scrambled Words With a Side of Toast Give each table group a phrase about good communication skills to unscramble. For example: gniltisne itwh cteersp (listening with respect); eginb nkid ot otsrhe (being kind to others); ktgian bystelirsiipon (taking responsibility). Each group discusses the importance of their phrase and creates a quote (the "toast") about their phrase that can inspire everyone in Advisory. Then each group shares their phrase and quote with the whole group.

Reflection Gather everyone in a circle. Ask: "Which quality or qualities would you like to work on as an Advisory team?"

DAY 2 ■ What We Have in Common

Arrival Welcome

Greet each student by name as they enter. Remind them to read the announcements message.

Announcements

> Welcome, Advisory Team!
>
> Today we're going to start learning about each other. Why? Because getting to know each other is how we're going to build a positive community for the year ahead.
>
> Write your responses to the following questions: What's your favorite food? What's your favorite TV show or movie? What's your favorite sport, game, or activity? Be prepared to share your responses with a partner.

Point out today's key school and team events.

Acknowledgments

Partner Chat Students pair up with another table group member. After greeting their partner by name, they take turns sharing their responses to the announcements prompt. Then partners introduce each other to their table group. Model the introduction: "This is _____. Her favorite food is _____, her favorite movie is _____, and her favorite sport is _____." Listen in on each group and note some favorites to use in future Advisory meetings.

Activity

Four Corners Pose one of the acknowledgments questions (for example, "What's your favorite food?") and designate each corner of the room as one response you heard students mention (for example, corner 1—pizza; 2—fruit; 3—ice cream; 4—tacos). Have students move to the corner that most closely represents their response and discuss why they made their choice. Repeat for the other two questions.

Reflection Gather everyone in a circle. Ask: "What did you notice about what people have in common?"

First Impressions

Make personal connections to Advisory group and learn Advisory routines

---

DAY 3 ▪ Our School Favorites

Arrival Welcome

Greet each student by name as they enter. Consider also shaking hands or giving a high five. Remind them to read the announcements message.

Announcements

> Hello, Advisory Team!
>
> Do you realize that you've been in school for more than half your life now? This year, if we build a supportive community, you'll each learn more and have more fun doing it!
>
> Think about your experiences as a student. Who were some favorite teachers? Classes? Activities? Be prepared to share one school favorite (and why) with your table group.

Point out today's key school and team events.

Acknowledgments

One-Sentence Sharing In their table group, students take turns introducing themselves and sharing one-sentence responses to the announcements prompt. For example: "I'm Martellus. My favorite teacher was Ms. Jackson in third grade because we did a lot of science experiments." Repeat for a few more rounds, as time allows. Listen in on each group and note some favorites.

Activity

Just Like Me Use what you heard from the table groups to create prompts. As you say each prompt, students who feel it applies to them stand up (or raise hands if standing is difficult) and say "Just like me" at the same time. Take time to observe who does not stand up (or who doesn't stand as often), and check in with them to hear their ideas. Repeat for as many rounds as time allows.

Just Like Me Prompt Ideas

- ➤ I like math.
- ➤ I like teachers who challenge me.
- ➤ I like team sports.

Reflection Gather everyone in a circle. Ask: "What do our school favorites have in common?"

DAY 4 ■ Reflecting on First Impressions

Arrival Welcome

Greet each student by name as they enter. Remind them to read the announcements message.

Announcements

Congratulations, Team!

We've made it through our first week of Advisory. Let's look back and then ahead. First impressions can make for lasting impressions, but they are not permanent.

Think back on your first impressions of our Advisory. What were they? Have your impressions changed, and if so, how? Be prepared to share with your table group.

Point out today's (and/or this weekend's) key school and team events.

Acknowledgments

Around-the-Table Sharing Students greet each of their tablemates by name and take turns sharing their response to the announcements prompt. After everyone has shared, students engage in a more free-flowing conversation. Circulate and listen in on each group; note some responses.

Activity

Fact or Fiction Students write three statements about themselves: two are factual (true); one is fictional (false). For example: "I moved here from Chicago [T]. My favorite ice cream is salted caramel [T]. I play basketball [F]." Then one student reads the statements aloud. The other students vote on which statement they think is false. The student who read reveals the false one. Continue until everyone has shared, or spread this activity over several Advisory meetings.

Reflection Gather everyone in a circle. Ask: "How important are first impressions? How much truth is in first impressions? How much should they influence how we treat others?"

Life Stories

Strengthen the Advisory community by sharing personal interests and learning about others

---

Skills Practiced This Week

Building positive relationships

Cooperation

Self-control

Self-reflection

Speaking essentials

Life Story Directions

Fold a piece of paper into six sections. Open the paper back up and name each section. For example: Section 1—favorite book character; 2—musical group you want to spend a day with; 3—a childhood memory; 4—an adult whom you really respect; 5—an activity you've never tried but would like to; 6—an ideal job or career.

DAY 1 ■ Getting to Know You, PART 1

Arrival Welcome

Greet each student by name as they enter. Remind students to read the announcements message.

Announcements

Welcome Back to Advisory!

Today we're going to learn more about each other by looking at what else we have in common.

Think about what you would do if you had one more day in the weekend.

Include upcoming school and team events in your messages this week.

Acknowledgments

Around-the-Table Hello At each table, the student whose birthday is closest to today's date goes first. This student greets the person to their right by name with a friendly "Hello," and the greeting is sent around the table. Once everyone has been greeted, students take turns responding to the announcements prompt. Encourage students to ask clarifying questions and discuss any commonalities they noticed.

Activity

Life Story Give each student a Life Story* sheet. Let students know they can brainstorm ideas with their table group while they work individually on their Life Story (see directions in margin). Give students 5 minutes to create their Life Story. Create your own Life Story and be the first to share #6 with the whole group. Then have each student share their #6 with the whole group. Have students put their name on their Life Story, and collect them to use again.

Reflection Gather everyone in a circle. Ask: "What are some things we have in common based only on what we shared about our Life Stories today?"

*A Life Story template is available to download; see page 19.

Arrival Welcome

Greet each student by name as they enter.

Announcements

> Hello, Advisory Team!
>
> Welcome back! Hopefully you've made some connections with others here in Advisory. Today you'll have an opportunity to make even more connections as we build our Advisory community.
>
> Get your Life Story, and sit with three students whom you did not sit with yesterday.

Point out today's key school and team events.

Acknowledgments

Life Story Section #5 Students take turns sharing with their tablemates their Life Story section about the activity they would like to try (#5). After each student shares, anyone who would like to try that activity says so. After a few minutes, ask three to five volunteers to share their activity, and see if students in the other table groups would also want to try it (you may want to go first to model this). Collect students' Life Stories to use again.

Activity

Four Corners Pose one of the questions listed in the margin (or one you created) and designate one corner of the room for each response. Give students time to think about their choice (or the option that is closest to their choice). Then signal for them to move to that corner and discuss their choice with a partner or small group there. Repeat for one or more questions and responses as time allows.

Reflection Gather everyone in a circle. Ask: "How do you think getting to know each other helps build a stronger Advisory community? Why is doing so important?"

Four Corners Examples

➡ If you had to eat one food for the rest of your life, what would it be?

1: Vegetables
2: Pasta
3: Chocolate
4: Fruit

➡ What's your favorite day of the week?

1: Friday
2: Saturday
3: Sunday
4: A different day

➡ If you could live anywhere, where would it be?

1: By the ocean
2: On a mountain
3: In a major city
4: In a small town

Life Stories

Strengthen the Advisory community by sharing personal interests and learning about others

Incorporations Sample Questions

→ When you get home from school, do you first do homework, eat a snack, or take time to relax?

→ Over the weekend, would you rather play games, exercise, watch movies, or visit relatives?

→ Is your birthday in the winter, spring, summer, or fall?

NOTE Collect everyone's Life Stories. Students will reference these in the "Life Stories, Take 2" Advisory week (pages 124-127).

DAY 3 ■ Getting to Know You, PART 3

Arrival Welcome

Greet each student by name as they enter. Encourage students to do a quick binder check as they get settled (see page 17).

Announcements

Hello, Storytellers,

Today you'll use your Life Story papers again. This time, you'll be sharing the story behind a childhood memory. Think about the details of that story, but keep these details to yourself. You'll see why soon.

Find your Life Story on a table—that's your seat for today.

Point out today's key school and team events.

Acknowledgments

Incorporations Ask a question that relates to students' lives. For example: "Are you the oldest, youngest, middle, or only child?" Designate a space in the room for each response. Students form groups in the space that matches their response and share one sentence about their response. Repeat with other questions (see sample questions in margin).

Activity

Fact or Fiction Students reference their childhood memory (#3) from their Life Story.* They write three statements about it: two are factual (true); one is fictional (false). For example: "On my first day of kindergarten, I wore a red shirt [T]. I spilled milk at lunch [F]. I got to use scissors for the first time [T]." Then one student reads their statement aloud. The other students vote on which statement they think is false. The student who read reveals the false one. Continue until everyone has shared, or spread this activity over several Advisories.

Reflection "What are some of the things that people's true statements have in common?"

*A Life Story template is available to download; see page 19.

DAY 4 ■ Getting to Know You, PART 4

Arrival Welcome

Greet each student by name as they enter. Consider also shaking hands or giving a fist bump.

Announcements

> Hi, Team!
>
> Wow! Time really does fly—it's already the end of another week together. You've learned a lot about each other in such a short time. Let's again look back and look ahead.
>
> Reflect on our Advisory meetings. What do you most enjoy about them?

Point out today's (and/or this weekend's) key school and team events.

Acknowledgments

Around-the-Table Sharing Students greet each of their tablemates by name. Then they take turns sharing briefly what they enjoy about Advisory, and why. After everyone has had a turn, they take turns sharing ideas about how to improve Advisory. Ask a volunteer from each table to summarize their group's ideas while you (or a student) records them for future reference.

Activity

Ball Toss Use any kind of squishy ball or beach ball. Students stand at their desks or in a circle. Call out a student's name and toss the ball to them. That student shares one enjoyable thing about Advisory, tosses the ball to another student, and sits down. The activity continues until everyone has had a turn or time is up.

Reflection Gather everyone in a circle. Ask: "Which idea for improving Advisory do you think we should try first, and why?"

All About Respect

Brainstorm and discuss what respect looks like in the school setting

---

Skills Practiced This Week

Active listening
Brainstorming
Respecting others
Self-awareness
Self-control

NOTE Brainwriting is brainstorming and writing down ideas before sharing them.

DAY 1 ■ R-E-S-P-E-C-T

Arrival Welcome

Greet each student by name as they enter. Remind students to read the announcements message. Consider having the song "Respect" (or a similar one) playing in the background.

Announcements

Welcome, Advisory Team!

You're going to delve into the meaning of respect this week. Check out this song lyric made famous by singer Aretha Franklin:

"All I'm askin' is for a little respect."

Think about what this quote means to you. Be prepared to share your thoughts with a partner.

Include upcoming school and team events in your messages this week.

Acknowledgments

Partner Chat In their table group, students pair up, greet their partner by name, and take turns sharing their responses to the announcements prompt. Then they summarize what their partner said with their table group. Ask two or three volunteers to share their table group's ideas with the whole group.

Activity

Encore Brainwriting Give small groups sticky notes and a large piece of paper; assign recorders for each group. Recorders make a T-chart on the paper and write "respect" in the left-hand column. Individually, students list songs that contain "respect" in the title or lyrics on a sticky note (one song per sticky note), and then post them in the left-hand column. Each group then discusses their personal connections to the songs; recorders summarize their group's connections in the right-hand column. Display the finished charts.

Reflection "Think about what respect means to you. Why do you think it's important that we treat everyone with respect?"

Respecting Peers, PART 1

Arrival Welcome

Greet each student by name as they enter. Encourage students to do a quick binder check as they get settled (see page 17).

Announcements

> Hello, Quote Makers,
>
> **Quote of the Day** "Deal with yourself as an individual worthy of respect and make everyone else deal with you the same way." —NIKKI GIOVANNI, POET
>
> Create your own quote about respect, write it down on a slip of paper or sticky note, and be prepared to share it with others.

Point out today's key school and team events.

Acknowledgments

Around-the-Table Chat Students greet each of their tablemates by name and then take turns reading their quotes aloud. Then they have a more free-flowing discussion about how to give and get respect from peers.

Activity

Silent Quotes Trade Students mix and mingle in silence and greet a partner by nodding or bowing. Then partners exchange their quotes, read them silently, and close their eyes to reflect on the quote for 10–15 seconds. Repeat as time allows. Collect all the quotes and read a few aloud.

Reflection Gather everyone in a circle. Ask: "What quote did you have the strongest connection to, and why? How can these quotes help us act, speak, and listen to our peers with more respect?"

All About Respect

Brainstorm and discuss what respect looks like in the school setting

DAY 3 ■ Respecting Peers, PART 2

Arrival Welcome

Greet each student by name as they enter.

Announcements

> Welcome, Team!
>
> We talked a lot about respect this week, and you came up with some great quotes yesterday. Today you're going to dig deeper and explore respect in action.
>
> Pick up a Respect LSF Chart. List what *you* think respect should **L**ook, **S**ound, and **F**eel like here at school with your peers.

Point out today's key school and team events.

 TIP

Meeting One-on-One With Your Advisees

You can use this time to pair up with one advisee to get to know them better and continue to strengthen your relationship with them.

Acknowledgments

Swap Meet Students mix and mingle, greeting each other with a handshake or low five. On your signal, students find a partner close to them and exchange ideas from their Respect LSF* chart. Encourage students to record any of their partner's ideas that they connect with. Repeat for two to four more rounds. Collect everyone's charts.

Activity

Museum Walk Display the completed Respect LSF Charts around the room or on tables. Have students walk around and review all the charts. As they do, they should draw a star next to any idea they connect with. Gather everyone together and invite volunteers to share their observations.

Reflection "Think about your daily interactions with your peers here. Think about all the ideas shared today. What concrete actions can you do to ensure you're truly treating others with respect?"

*An LSF Chart template is available to download; see page 19.

Respect Street

Arrival Welcome

Greet each student by name as they enter. Consider also shaking hands or giving a fist bump.

Announcements

> Congratulations, Team!
>
> You've done some hard (and fun) work digging deeper into what respect is all about and ways to treat everyone with more respect.
>
> Ponder this: How is respect like a street? (For example: Respect is like a street because it goes in both directions.)

Point out today's (and/or this weekend's) key school and team events.

Acknowledgments

Making Connections In their table group, students greet each other and then brainstorm possible connections (serious or silly) between "street" and "respect," coming up with valid reasons to support their connections.

Activity

Amazing Analogies Write the following on chart paper or a whiteboard: "Respect is like a street because _____." Each group chooses one of their connections to create their own analogy similar to the example in the announcements prompt. Have each group share their analogy with the whole group. Post everyone's analogies.

Reflection "Think about a highway, a byway, and an avenue. The highway is a positive experience you had this week, the byway is an off-track experience you had this week, and the avenue is something you're looking forward to this weekend." Invite a few students to share their highway, byway, or avenue with the whole group.

Inspiring Others

Examine how teamwork and positive actions promote individual and group success

Skills Practiced This Week

Analyzing
Building community
Leadership
Problem-solving
Teamwork

Graffiti Headings

➡ What's the difference between a team and a clique?

➡ What does being part of a team look, sound, and feel like?

➡ What advice would you give Indigo?

➡ How do you include others in your daily life at school?

DAY 1 ■ Making Us a Stronger Team, PART 1

Arrival Welcome

Greet each student by name as they enter. Remind students to read the announcements message.

Announcements

Welcome, Advisory Team!

You've probably all experienced or witnessed a team getting better over time and a team getting worse or even falling apart. What made the difference?

Indigo's Story Indigo loved basketball, so she was thrilled when she made the junior varsity team as a 9th grader. But she was ready to quit by the end of the season because of the cliques that had formed and divided the team.

What advice would you give Indigo?

Include school and team events in your messages this week

Acknowledgments

What's Your Advice? One student in each table group begins by greeting the student to their left with "Good morning, Desiree. What's your advice?" That student returns the greeting and shares their advice. Continue around the table until everyone has shared their advice.

Activity

Graffiti Post chart paper with the headings shown at left. Invite students to "graffiti" their ideas on the charts (starting at any chart, going in any order, writing in any style anywhere on the chart). Have table groups find common themes among the ideas on each chart. Then have each group share their findings with the whole group.

Reflection "Rate your contribution as a team member in today's activity from 1 (low) to 5 (high). Why did you give yourself that rating? How important is each individual team member to a team's success?"

DAY 2 ▪ Making Us a Stronger Team, PART 2

Arrival Welcome

Greet each student by name as they enter. Consider adding in a handshake or a high five.

Announcements

> It's a Terrific Tuesday, Team!
>
> A disagreement or difference of opinion can divide a team—or bring it closer together. What makes the difference?
>
> **Isaiah's Story** Isaiah was named one of the student band leaders. But he and the other two leaders couldn't agree on how to run the band's fundraising event. With only 1 week left to plan, Isaiah believed the event would be a disaster because there was still so much to do.
>
> On sticky notes, write down 3 pieces of advice you'd give Isaiah. You can reference yesterday's graffiti charts for ideas.

Point out today's key school and team events.

Acknowledgments

What's Your Advice? One student in each table group begins by greeting the student to their left with "Good morning, Felix. What's your advice?" That student returns the greeting and shares their advice. Continue around the table until everyone has shared their advice. Then have a few students share a summary of their group's ideas with the whole group. Add Isaiah's name to the "What advice would you give Indigo?" graffiti chart and have students add their sticky notes from the announcements prompt.

Activity

Body Drumming Have students stand and spread out so that they have room to do the motions safely. See margin for Body Drumming directions.

Reflection Ask: "What are three ways we can make our Advisory team stronger in the next week or so?"

Body Drumming Directions

First teach and practice a three-count stomp-and-clap pattern: Stomp, stomp, clap! Stomp, stomp, clap! Then teach and practice a four-count pattern: Stomp, stomp, stomp, clap! Stomp, stomp, stomp, clap!

Divide the class in half and assign one half the three-count pattern and the other half the four-count pattern. On your signal, the two groups perform their pattern simultaneously. After 1–2 minutes, signal for all students to stop at the same time. Repeat.

To add challenge, create more elaborate drumming patterns.

Inspiring Others

Examine how team-work and positive actions promote individual and group success

DAY 3 ▪ The Music of Inspiration

Arrival Welcome

Greet each student by name as they enter. Encourage students to do a quick binder check as they get settled (see page 17). Consider playing soft music.

Announcements

> Dear Music Lovers,
>
> Think about the people who create the songs we listen to. Do you think songs with a positive message are as popular as those with a not-so-positive message?
>
> List 3 songs you like that have a positive message.

Point out today's key school and team events.

Acknowledgments

Finding Common Themes Students greet their tablemates by name, offering a handshake or a gentle fist bump. Then each student shares their three songs and why they connect to these songs with their group. Each group lists common themes among their songs, such as friendship or courage. One reporter from each table then shares these themes with the whole group.

Activity

Encore Choose one of the themes from those shared during acknowledgments. In their table group, students brainstorm which of their group's songs relate to that theme; then each reporter shares their group's list of songs with the whole group. Record these, or ask a student to do so. In turn, each table group chooses one song and, without revealing the title, hums a few bars. The rest of the students try to guess the name of the song and its artist. Repeat so that each table group has a chance to hum at least once.

Reflection "How can music inspire you? Inspire others?"

DAY 4 ■ Inspiring Others

Arrival Welcome

Greet each student by name as they enter.

Announcements

> Hello, Inspirational Team!
>
> **Quote of the Day** "Our chief want is for someone to inspire us to be what we know we can be." —RALPH WALDO EMERSON, WRITER, PHILOSOPHER
>
> Think about your experiences in school this week. Who or what has inspired you? Be prepared to share your ideas.

Point out today's (and/or this weekend's) key school and team events.

Acknowledgments

Inside-Outside Circles Students count off by twos. Ones form an inner circle and face out; twos form an outer circle and face in to form pairs. Partners greet each other by name and share one or two sentences about who or what has inspired them this week. Then twos move one person to their right and greet their new partner. Continue for several rounds.

Activity

Quote Makers Working with a partner or in small groups, students create at least one quote that will serve to inspire other students to do their best. Invite each pair or group to write their quote on a chart and add decorations or design flair. Encourage students to present or display their quotes for the school community (for example, at an assembly, on a bulletin board, or on the school website).

Reflection Gather everyone in a circle. Have students reflect on their efforts as a team during Advisory this week. Ask: "How will you stay strong as a team next week? How will you stay inspired next week?"

End-of-Year Celebration

Look back on the year in Advisory and look forward to next year

---

Skills Practiced This Week

Building positive relationships

Goal setting

Self-motivation

Summarizing

Visualization

DAY 1 ▪ Advisory Pride

Arrival Welcome

Greet each student by name as they enter. Remind students to read the announcements message.

Announcements

> Welcome, Team!
>
> It's the last week of school! You've worked so hard all year, and it's really paid off.
>
> **Quote of the Day** "Memories are keys not to the past, but to the future."
> —CORRIE TEN BOOM, HELPED JEWS ESCAPE THE HOLOCAUST
>
> What's one favorite Advisory memory from this year? Be ready to share.

Include upcoming school and team events in your messages this week.

Acknowledgments

What's the News? In their table group, one student begins by greeting the student to their left by saying "Good morning, _____. What's the news?" The student greeted responds with "Good morning, _____. The news is [student shares their response to the announcements prompt]." Continue around the table until all students have been greeted and have shared their memory. Invite a few volunteers to share their favorite memory with the whole group.

Activity

Scrambled Words With a Side of Toast Give each table group a phrase about the success of Advisory to unscramble. For example: ahrd kowr sypa fof (hard work pays off); grtsno yummnocit (strong community). Then have each group discuss the importance of their phrase as it relates to Advisory and create a quote (the "toast") about their phrase that highlights what they're most proud of in Advisory. Have each group share their phrase and quote with the whole group.

Reflection Gather everyone in a circle. Ask: "What does the Quote of the Day mean to you? How might your favorite Advisory memories help you in the new school year?"

DAY 2 ■ Summer Plans

Arrival Welcome

Greet each student by name as they enter. Consider adding in a handshake or a high five.

Announcements

> Hi, Sunny Students!
>
> Everyone take a deep breath and let it out. The year is almost over, and soon you'll be on summer break.
>
> What is something you're looking forward to this summer? Why? Be ready to share.

Point out today's key school and team events.

Acknowledgments

One-Sentence Sharing Students count off to form groups of four. They greet each other by name, passing a friendly "Hello" and a high five around the group, and then take turns sharing a one-sentence response to the announcements prompt.

Activity

Solar Power Explain that this visualization exercise will help students relax and that they can do it anytime, anywhere. Have students stand at their desks or in a circle, close their eyes, and take a few slow, deep breaths. Lead the class in the guided visualization shown at left.

Reflection "What helps you construct vivid pictures in your mind? How can creating positive mental images help people relax when they're feeling overwhelmed, anxious, or stressed?"

Solar Power Directions

"Imagine the sun is just above you. Visualize the sun's light and energy slowly filling your head, then moving gently into your neck, spreading into your shoulders . . . your arms . . . your hands . . . your legs . . . your feet. Imagine the warm light filling your whole body. Now imagine the sun's warmth and light shining out of you. You can share the sun's light and energy— your own personal solar power—any time you want to relax or refocus. Now take a slow, deep breath . . . and open your eyes."

End-of-Year Celebration

Look back on the year in Advisory and look forward to next year

DAY 3 ▪ Preparing for the Next School Year

Arrival Welcome

Greet each student by name as they enter. Encourage students to do a quick binder check as they get settled (see page 17).

Announcements

Hello, Strategists!

Thought for Today When you prepare for the future, you're preparing for success.

What can you do over the summer to prepare for the next school year? Be ready to share.

Point out today's key school and team events.

Acknowledgments

Mix and Mingle to Music Play upbeat music as students walk around the room. When you stop the music, students greet another student by name and offer a fist bump or some other friendly gesture. Then they exchange responses from the announcements prompt. After 30 seconds, start the music again. Repeat so students greet at least four or five classmates; then they return to their table group.

Activity

World Café* Assign each table group a facilitator, and give them an index card with a strategy on it (for example, create a summer reading list). Students discuss ideas for each strategy (for example, read two books a month). After 2–3 minutes, signal to wrap up conversations. Everyone except the facilitator changes tables. The facilitator summarizes the previous group's ideas, and then the new group discusses their own ideas.

Reflection Gather everyone in a circle. Ask: "What is one idea that really stuck out to you? How can this knowledge help you prepare for next year?"

*This is an adaptation of the World Café™, a structured conversational process found at www.theworldcafe.com.

DAY 4 ■ Celebrating the Year Together

Arrival Welcome
Greet each student by name as they enter.

Announcements

> Greetings, Advisory Team!
>
> Think about the many things we've learned and accomplished as a team. Let's celebrate our year together.
>
> What's one thing you learned this year about working together as a team in Advisory? Be ready to share.

Point out today's (and/or this summer's) key school and team events.

Acknowledgments

One-Minute Greeting Students greet as many people by name as they can in one minute. When time is up, they partner with the last person they greeted and share their response to the announcements prompt. Invite a few volunteers to share their partner's response.

Activity

Let It Rain Students stand in a circle or by their desks. Say: "I'm the storm maestro. When I do an action, copy me, and we'll replicate a rainstorm together." Without talking, lead students through the rainstorm as it builds (see directions at left). Then challenge everyone to make the rain get softer as the storm dies down (do directions in reverse).

Reflection "Looking back on this year, list three big ideas that you learned in Advisory, two questions that you still have, and one takeaway or practical tip that you plan to put into action next year."

Let It Rain Directions

Rub hands on thighs (light wind)

Rub hands together (stronger wind)

Snap fingers (soft rain)

Clap hands softly (hard rain)

Clap hands loudly (pouring rain)

Slap thighs loudly (soft thunder)

Stomp feet (loud thunder)

Support Academic Readiness

4-Day Plans

Tips for Supporting Academic Readiness

All Grades

Middle school students need to learn in ways that are both active and interactive. Plan activities that are hands-on, experiential, social, and collaborative that focus on academic learning skills such as academic mindset, academic perseverance, academic behaviors, and learning strategies. Also, use brain breaks to help students stay focused and energized so that they can better absorb what they're learning.

Help students get organized and invested in their learning by having them set SMART goals. SMART goals are specific, measurable, achievable, realistic, and time-bound. Whenever a new quarter begins, look for opportunities to give students time to reflect on their progress and revise current goals or set new ones.

Grade Six

Learning to take responsibility for their homework can be a challenge, so most students will benefit from some explicit teaching and ongoing support with time-management and homework skills, especially organizational skills.

This group can struggle to make good decisions, so provide opportunities to discuss the pros and cons of issues. Most students enjoy debating, but they'll need support in developing this skill in positive ways, such as through focused debates on issues of interest to them.

Use this age group's natural desire to learn new content and skills when helping them revise existing goals or set new ones (rather than focusing on reviewing or revisiting old content/skills).

Grade Seven

This age group is capable of self-awareness and empathy, so allow them time to connect with each other, reflect on their challenges and achievements, and plan for future work. They may have worked on time-management and organizational skills last year, but some extra support early in the year may go a long way.

Seventh graders are able to see both sides of an argument, which serves them well in classroom debates. Connecting issues that are relevant to their lives to discussions and projects will help support their social and cognitive growth.

Grade Eight

This age group can exert a lot of peer pressure on others while feeling peer pressure more strongly internally, too. Because their cognitive abilities are advancing, they can consider different sides of an issue and multiple solutions more rationally and thoughtfully.

Students may want to take fewer academic risks. They'll especially benefit from keeping their routines as predictable as possible.

At this age, students can be excited one minute and bored the next, highly motivated and then withdrawn and lacking confidence. Encouraging them to see themselves as capable, productive people can go a long way toward helping them reach their goals.

Goal for Gold

Set academic goals and create concrete plans to achieve them

Skills Practiced This Week

Goal-setting
Responsibility
Self-motivation
Teamwork
Time management

TIP Tell students that the key to reaching a goal is creating a plan to support it. Explain that they will begin creating that plan today by turning their goal into a SMART goal: Specific, Measurable, Achievable, Relevant, and Time-Bound.

DAY 1 ▪ Setting Goals

Arrival Welcome

Greet each student by name as they enter. Remind students to read the announcements message.

Announcements

Welcome, Goal Setters!

This week you're going to set goals for the 1st semester and create an action plan to achieve them.

A Goal Story, Part 1 At age 8, Michael had a goal: "I would like to make the Olympics." Years later, when he was a teenager, Michael made the team. You'll learn more about Michael tomorrow.

Think about a goal you'd like to achieve in a class over the next 3 weeks. Be ready to share.

Include upcoming school and team events in your messages this week.

Acknowledgments

Partner Chat At tables, students greet each other by name. Then they partner up to share their response to the announcements prompt. If time allows, students share their partner's goal with their table group.

Activity

Creating a SMART Goal Give each student a SMART goal* sheet, and coach them in writing their goal in the first box. (Example of a SMART goal: "I want to get a B on the next math test.") Collect the SMART goal sheets to use again.

Reflection "How does setting a SMART goal differ from simply saying 'I hope I pass my math test'?"

*A SMART goal template is available to download; see page 19.

DAY 2 ■ Planning How to Reach a Goal

Guided Brainstorming Directions

- Each table group defines "effort" in their own words and shares the definition with the whole group. Facilitate reaching a whole-group consensus definition of "effort."

- With the consensus definition as a guide, students record four efforts that will help them progress toward their goal. For example: "If my goal is a B on the math test, one effort I can make is to study math for 15 more minutes each night."

- Each table group discusses how effort relates to change and shares their ideas with the whole group. Find commonalities among ideas, and emphasize the connection between effort and change.

- Students record four small changes that are likely to result if they put in their four efforts. For example: "If I study math for 15 more minutes each night, I expect to understand the chapter content better."

Arrival Welcome

Greet each student by name as they enter.

Announcements

Hello, Action Planners!

Today we're going to create a plan of action so you can reach your SMART goal. There are two parts to this plan: Effort and Small Changes.

A Goal Story, Part 2 Through thousands of hours of practice, Michael made four more Olympic teams and ended up winning the most Olympic medals in history. Maybe you remember him—Michael Phelps.

Get your SMART goal sheet from yesterday and review it. Sit with your table group and chat about the connection between effort and change.

Point out today's key school and team events.

Acknowledgments

What's the News? In their table group, one student begins by greeting the student to their left by saying "Good morning, _____. What's the news?" The student greeted responds with "Good morning, _____. The news is I have set a goal to [student shares goal from their SMART goal sheet]." Continue around the table until all students have been greeted and have shared their goal.

Activity

Creating a SMART Goal Plan Students stay in their table groups and use their SMART goal sheet from Day 1. Through guided brainstorming (see directions in margin), they explore this question together: "How does effort lead to change?" Then they complete the middle two columns on their SMART goal sheet. Collect the SMART goal sheets to use again.

Reflection Ask students to share with their table group one "aha" moment they had about effort leading to change while creating their SMART goal plan.

Goal for Gold

Set academic goals and create concrete plans to achieve them

Hand Up, Pair Up Directions

Round 1: Students find a partner from a different table group, give a high five, and share their SMART goal* and one effort they listed.

Round 2: Students find a partner from a different table group, give a high five, and share their goal and one small change they listed.

Rounds 3 and 4: Students find a partner from a different table group, give a high five, and share their goal and one challenge or barrier that might get in the way of reaching their goal.

> **NOTE** Collect everyone's Life Stories. Students will reference these in the "Goals Revisited" Advisory week (pages 62–65).

DAY 3 ▪ Hurdling Barriers to Reaching Goals

Arrival Welcome

Greet each student by name as they enter. Encourage students to do a quick binder check as they get settled (see page 17).

Announcements

Welcome, Goal Setters!

Quote of the Day "If you have a positive attitude and constantly strive to give your best effort, eventually you will overcome your immediate problems and find you are ready for greater challenges." —PAT RILEY, PRO BASKETBALL EXECUTIVE

Get your SMART goal sheet from yesterday and review it. Sit with your table group from yesterday.

Point out today's key school and team events.

Acknowledgments

Hand Up, Pair Up Follow the directions at left.

Activity

Carousel As a whole group, brainstorm hurdles (barriers) that get in the way of reaching goals. List the top five or six ideas on chart paper (one idea per chart), and post these around the room. With their table group, students rotate to each chart, brainstorm ideas for overcoming that hurdle, and list their group's ideas on the chart. Signal when it's time for groups to rotate to keep things moving and to ensure that all groups contribute ideas to each chart. Discuss the ideas for overcoming hurdles as time allows.

Reflection Have students review each chart on their own. Ask: "Which of these hurdles could get in the way of reaching your goal? What are some ways you can leap over them?"

DAY 4 ■ Goal Support

Arrival Welcome

Greet each student by name as they enter. Consider also giving a fist bump or a high ten.

Announcements

> Go, Team, Go!
>
> You've set goals, made plans for reaching them, and figured out ways to leap over hurdles that get in your way. Sometimes, you still might stumble or even get tripped up. Ouch! When that happens, supportive teammates can help pick you up and keep you on track to reach the finish line!
>
> Think about a time when you worked successfully as part of a team or group. What were 2 or 3 keys to your success? Be ready to share.

Point out today's (and/or this weekend's) key school and team events.

Acknowledgments

Keys to Success Students greet their tablemates and then take turns sharing their responses to the announcements prompt.

Activity

Keys to Success Performance Students brainstorm with their tablemates how they might apply their keys to success to future goals. Each table group creates a rap (or song or very brief skit) based on their keys to success brainstorming session and performs it for the whole group. If there isn't enough time for all groups to perform, spread out this activity over a few days.

Reflection Gather everyone in a circle. Ask: "What made your performance fun and successful? How can you use what you learned today to support one another in reaching your goals?"

Keys to Success Examples

➤ "Working through problems together."

➤ "Listening to one another."

➤ "Giving everyone an equal chance to express their ideas and opinions."

➤ "Doing my fair share of the work."

Effort Equals Success

Learn how effort, persistence, and personal responsibility lead to academic success

Skills Practiced This Week

Evaluating

Perseverance

Responsibility

Summarizing

Graffiti Headings

➤ What is effort?

➤ What is success in school?

➤ How does effort determine success in school?

➤ How can you improve your effort?

DAY 1 ▪ Building an Academic Mindset

Arrival Welcome

Greet each student by name as they enter. Remind students to read the announcements message.

Announcements

Welcome, Hardworking Students!

What does it mean to be successful? Does success just happen, or do you make it happen?

Tanya's Story Tanya believed she wasn't smart, so she didn't put much effort into her schoolwork. Then her fifth grade teacher taught her a simple equation: Effort = Success. Since then, Tanya has worked hard and asks for extra help when she needs it. She now feels successful as a student because she advocates for herself and persists in reaching her goals.

Think about what the equation Effort = Success means to you. Be prepared to share your ideas with a partner.

Include upcoming school and team events in your messages this week.

Acknowledgments

Partner Chat At tables, students greet each other by name. With a partner, students share their responses to the announcements prompt, and then summarize their partner's ideas for their tablemates.

Activity

Graffiti Post chart paper around the room with the headings shown at left. Students "graffiti" their ideas on the charts (starting at any chart, going in any order, and writing in any style anywhere on the chart). Then assign small groups to find common themes among the ideas on the charts, and have each group share a summary of their findings. Keep the charts posted for this week's Advisory meetings.

Reflection "Rate your effort in today's Advisory from 1 (low) to 5 (high). Why did you give yourself that rating? How would you rate everyone's effort as a group? How does individual effort connect to group effort and group success?"

DAY 2 ■ Developing Grit

Arrival Welcome

Greet each student by name as they enter. Consider adding in a handshake or a high five.

Announcements

> It's a Gritty Tuesday!
>
> Grit is about sticking with a task or an assignment and finishing it. It's about working at something even when the work gets harder.
>
> **Marc's Story** Marc has always done OK in school, but this year he's struggling in math. When he gets stuck on a problem, he gets very frustrated and finds himself giving up.
>
> On sticky notes, write down 3 pieces of advice you'd give Marc.

Point out today's key school and team events.

Acknowledgments

What's Your Advice? One student in each table group begins by greeting the student to their right with "Good morning, Jacqui. What's your advice?" That student returns the greeting and shares their advice. Continue around the table until everyone has shared their advice. Then have students add their sticky notes from the announcements prompt to the "How can you improve your effort?" graffiti chart they made yesterday.

Activity

Number Freeze Everyone begins sitting. Call out a target number—less than the total number of students but more than one-third the number. (For example, if there are 17 students present, pick a number between 6 and 16.) Continue with the directions at left.

Reflection "How do you think effort, persistence, and success are related?"

Number Freeze Directions

Set a timer for 60 seconds and say "Go!" Students try to get the target number of people to stand at the same time, following these rules: No one may talk or point; anyone may stand at any time, but no one may stand for more than 5 seconds at a time (students count to 5 silently). When you think the target number has been reached (or when the timer goes off), say "Freeze!" Students stay in position while you count those standing to see if the numbers match. Repeat with a new number.

Effort Equals Success

Learn how effort, persistence, and personal responsibility lead to academic success

---

DAY 3 ■ Taking Responsibility for Learning

Arrival Welcome

Greet each student by name as they enter. Encourage students to do a quick binder check as they get settled (see page 17).

Announcements

> Welcome, Team!
>
> Like respect, "responsibility" is a word we hear a lot about from teachers, coaches, and other adults at school.
>
> **Taylor's Story** Maybe you know someone like Taylor: He's a good student and teammate, but sometimes he speaks without thinking and doesn't seem to care if his words hurt others.
>
> If you were Taylor's friend, what would you say or do to help him take responsibility for his hurtful words?

Point out today's key school and team events.

Acknowledgments

Standing Partner Chat Have students stand up, pair up, and spread out throughout the room. After greeting their partner by name, they take turns sharing their responses to the announcements prompt.

Activity

Four Corners (variation) Post a chart in each corner of the room, labeled Responsible Friend, Responsible Student, Responsible Family Member, and Responsible Community Member. Assign a group of students to each corner. Each group lists their key ideas of what being responsible looks, sounds, and feels like for their category, and then rotates to the next corner and adds to that chart's list. Wrap up by discussing each chart as a whole group.

Reflection "What three specific actions might you take to become a more responsible student and/or friend? How might these actions also help you become a more responsible family member and community member?"

DAY 4 ■ Homework Helpers

Arrival Welcome

Greet each student by name as they enter.

Announcements

> Dear Homework Helpers,
>
> Think about your experiences with homework so far this year. What's gone well for you? What could be improved on?
>
> Be prepared to share some of your successes and challenges with homework so far this school year.

Point out today's (and/or this weekend's) key school and team events.

Acknowledgments

Inside-Outside Circles Students count off by twos. Ones form an inner circle and face out; twos form an outer circle and face in to form pairs. Partners greet each other by name and share one sentence about a homework success and one sentence about a challenge. Then twos move one person to their right and greet their new partner. Continue until everyone is back with their first partner. Make note of some successes and challenges students share.

Activity

Just Like Me Use what you heard from Inside-Outside Circles for prompts. As you say each prompt, students who feel it applies to them stand up (or raise hands if standing is difficult) and say "Just like me" at the same time. Take time to observe who does not stand (or who doesn't stand as often), and check in with them to hear their ideas. Repeat for as many rounds as time allows.

> **Just Like Me Prompt Ideas**
>
> ➜ I'm having a hard time keeping up with my reading in English.
>
> ➜ I try to take good notes in class because they help me study.
>
> ➜ I ask my teacher for help when I need it.

Reflection Have students reflect on the successes and challenges they heard. Consider listing these. Encourage students to create "Homework Helpers" anchor charts to post throughout the room or to keep in their notebooks for future reference.

Goals Revisited

Practice debate skills, and brainstorm ways to overcome distractions in pursuit of goals

Skills Practiced This Week

Goal-setting
Organization
Self-awareness
Staying focused
Time management

Three-Person Machine Example

Car wash: Two students stand facing each other a few feet apart. They act as the washer by raising their hands overhead and wiggling their fingers to mimic water falling over the "car." The third student pantomimes driving the car while walking slowly between them.

DAY 1 ▪ Thinking on Your Feet

Arrival Welcome

Greet each student by name as they enter. Remind students to read the announcements message.

Announcements

> Hello, Advisory Team,
>
> Today you'll be "thinking on your feet." That's kind of an odd-sounding expression, but quick thinking is a powerful skill to have!
>
> Find someone to quietly discuss this question with: How can thinking on your feet help you learn and make better decisions?

Include upcoming school and team events in your messages this week.

Acknowledgments

Pros and Cons Assign partners and have them decide who will start out as the caller and who will be the responder. State a topic (for example, wind power, energy drinks, or video games). Set a timer for 20 seconds and signal to begin. The caller claps hands and says "Pro!" The responder quickly names positive points about the topic. Set the timer for another 20 seconds and signal to begin. The caller claps hands again and says "Con!" The responder now names negative points about the topic.

For the next round, students keep the same partners but switch roles (use the same topic or state a new one). To wrap up, invite each pair to share one pro and one con, and then review these pros and cons as a whole group.

Activity

Three-Person Machine As a whole group, brainstorm different machines and tools used in daily life and list these ideas on chart paper. Students break into groups of three and brainstorm how to pantomime a machine from the list. Each group then demonstrates their machine for the rest of the students to guess.

Reflection "What made Pros and Cons successful? Three-Person Machine? How is being able to think on your feet a useful skill to have?"

DAY 2 ▪ Debate Training

Arrival Welcome

Greet each student by name as they enter. Consider also giving a fist bump or a low five.

Announcements

> Dear Debate Team,
>
> What goes into having a fair debate? Both sides need the same chance to make their case. What else?
>
> Think about the speaking and listening skills needed for a fair debate. List 3 of these skills. Refer to your list during Advisory today.

Point out today's key school and team events.

Acknowledgments

Maître d' Call out a table grouping (for example, "Table for 3!"). Students quickly form new standing groups of that number to discuss their responses to a question you pose (see example in margin). Give students 1–2 minutes to share. Repeat as time allows, continuing to vary the table size.

Maître d' Examples

→ **Table for 3:** What do you like most about middle school and why?

→ **Table for 2:** What do you like least about middle school and why?

→ **Table for 4:** If you could add any subject in school, what would it be and why?

Activity

Debate Duos In groups of four, two students are the "pros" (pair A), and two are the "cons" (pair B). State a topic (use topics related to questions you asked in Maître d'). Give students think time, then set a timer for 30 seconds and signal to begin. Pair A takes turns naming pros about the topic. After 30 seconds, signal to stop. Reset the timer and signal pair B to take turns naming cons about the topic. Signal again to end this round. For the next round, keep the same groups but have pairs switch roles, and state a new topic.

Reflection Gather everyone in a circle. Ask: "What listening and speaking skills did you use today? If you were to have a class debate in one of your core subjects, what key listening and speaking skills would you need to use for your debate to go well?"

Goals Revisited

Practice debate skills, and brainstorm ways to overcome distractions in pursuit of goals

DAY 3 ▪ Revisiting Our Goals

Arrival Welcome

Greet each student by name as they enter. Encourage students to do a quick binder check as they get settled (see page 17).

Announcements

Welcome, Progress Makers!

We're nearing the end of the first quarter. This is a great time to review your SMART goal plan and do a self-check on your progress. And if you've already reached your goal, congrats! Now's a great time to set some new goals.

Get your SMART goal sheet. On a sticky note, write down your distractors—things that get in the way of making progress toward your goals. Be ready to share.

Point out today's key school and team events.

Acknowledgments

Around-the-Table Sharing In their table group, students greet each other by name, and go around the table to share something new from their personal lives. Then they share what they wrote down for the announcements prompt.

Activity

Distract-a-thon Display everyone's distractors from the announcements prompt. Tell students that like a telethon or walkathon (which raises money for a charitable cause), this activity is designed to help them "raise" tips for overcoming goal distractors. Working in pairs, students choose a distractor (such as spending time on their phone instead of doing homework) and write tips for how to overcome it. The goal for this Distract-a-thon: Students write down as many tips for as many distractors as possible within the time limit you set. When time is up, count the total number of tips, read a few aloud, and display everyone's advice for future use.

NOTE Students will reference their SMART goal* sheets from the "Goal for Gold" Advisory week on pages 54–57.

Reflection "Take a look at your SMART goal again. Which tips do you think will help you avoid distractors and stay on track to reach your goals?" Collect everyone's SMART goals. Students will use these in tomorrow's Advisory.

*A SMART goal template is available to download; see page 19.

DAY 4 ■ Revising Goals or Making New Ones

Arrival Welcome

Greet each student by name as they enter.

Announcements

> Hello, Goal Setters!
>
> Yesterday you "raised" a lot of terrific tips for overcoming goal distractors! Today we'll use those tips to revise our existing goals or create new ones.
>
> Get your SMART goal sheet, and pick up a new blank one. Think about whether you want to revise an existing goal, create a new one, or both.

Point out today's (and/or this weekend's) key school and team events.

Acknowledgments

Hand Up, Pair Up Students walk around the room with one hand up. When they find a partner, they high-five, greet each other by name, and share their thoughts on the prompt you give. Students find a new partner for each round. Round 1: Share an update on your SMART goal progress. Round 2: Share one or more distractors that slowed your progress. Round 3: Share two ideas you plan to try for overcoming your distractors.

Activity

Part 1: Revising SMART Goals/Creating New Ones Guide students, individually or in pairs, in revising their SMART goals or creating new ones.

Part 2: Elevens In small groups, students stand with one hand behind their backs and say in unison: "One, two, three—eleven!" On "eleven," they silently throw their hands into the center as they flash any number of fingers, from zero (a fist) to five, to try to total eleven fingers. If the total of fingers doesn't equal eleven, they try again. If the total does equal eleven, the group joins another group and continues playing.

Reflection "What additional steps can you take to help you reach your goals?"

TIP

Meeting One-on-One With Your Advisees

You can use this time to pair up with one advisee to get to know them better and continue to strengthen your relationship with them.

NOTE Collect the SMART goals to use in the "Setting New Goals" Advisory week on pages 66–69.

Setting New Goals

Set new goals or revise old ones, and incorporate new habits for reaching them

---

Skills Practiced This Week

Asking for help
Goal-setting
Self-confidence
Self-reflection
Time management

NOTE Students will reference their SMART goal sheets from the "Goals Revisited" Advisory week on pages 62–65.

DAY 1 ▪ Setting New Goals

Arrival Welcome

Greet each student by name as they enter. Remind students to read the announcements message.

Announcements

Hello, Goal Setters!

This week we'll be talking about revising goals, setting new ones, and staying motivated.

Sally's Story, Part 1 Sally was studying physics when she saw an ad in her college newspaper calling for women to apply to the NASA astronaut program. She applied after graduation, and was one of six women chosen out of thousands of applicants.

Think back on your goals from last quarter. Do you want to revise those goals or make new ones for this new quarter? Be ready to share.

Include upcoming school and team events in your messages this week.

Acknowledgments

Partner Chat At tables, students form pairs, greet their partner by name, and ask for each other's thoughts about Sally's Story. Pairs then ask each other about their responses to the announcements prompt. Then they summarize what their partner said for their table group.

Activity

SMART Goals—Revising Old/Setting New Hand out new SMART goal sheets,* and coach students in revising their goals from last quarter or writing new ones. (Limit students to completing the first box; they can complete the rest of the boxes during this week's Advisory.)

Reflection "If you didn't reach your goals, what will you do differently to reach them this quarter? If you did reach your goals, what did you learn that will help you reach your goals for this quarter?"

*A SMART goal template is available to download; see page 19.

DAY 2 ■ Goals Confidence Boost

Guided Brainstorming Directions

Guided Brainstorming Directions

➤ Each table group defines "effort" in their own words and shares the definition with the whole group. Facilitate reaching a whole-group consensus definition of "effort."

➤ With the consensus definition as a guide, students record four efforts that will help them progress toward their goal. For example: "If my goal is a B on the math test, one effort I can make is to study math for 15 more minutes each night."

➤ Each table group discusses how effort relates to change and shares their ideas with the whole group. Find commonalities among ideas, and emphasize the connection between effort and change.

➤ Students record four small changes that are likely to result if they put in their four efforts. For example: "If I study math for 15 more minutes each night, I expect to understand the chapter content better."

Arrival Welcome

As students enter, greet each one by name and ask: "How confident do you feel about reaching your goals for this quarter—thumbs up, down, middle (so-so)?"

Announcements

Hello, Confident Learners!

When you make an effort, you tend to gain confidence, and this boost in confidence can help you work toward your goals.

Sally's Story, Part 2 After completing NASA's program, Sally started her aeronautics career as a ground-support crew member for NASA's second and third shuttle flights, serving as capsule communicator.

Get your SMART goal sheet from yesterday and review it. Think about the role self-confidence plays in reaching goals. Be prepared to share.

Point out today's key school and team events.

Acknowledgments

Around-the-Table Sharing Students greet each of their tablemates by name and take turns briefly sharing their responses to the announcements prompt. After everyone has had a turn to speak, they can have a more free-flowing conversation.

Activity

Creating a SMART Goal Plan Students complete the two middle columns of their SMART goal sheet individually. Then through guided brainstorming (see directions in margin), they explore ways they can put in more effort toward achieving their SMART goal. Give them a few minutes to revise their sheets based on their discussions, and then collect the SMART goal sheets. Students will use these during the "Goals, Take 3" Advisory week on pages 74–77.

Reflection Ask a few volunteers to share with the whole group one "aha" moment they had while creating or discussing their SMART goal plan.

Setting New Goals

Set new goals or revise old ones, and incorporate new habits for reaching them

DAY 3 ■ Keys to Success in Reaching Goals

Arrival Welcome

Greet each student by name as they enter. Encourage students to do a quick backpack check (clean them out, reorganize them, and so on).

Announcements

Dear Hardworking Team,

There are many keys to success that can help us reach our goals. You just have to look for them along the way.

Sally's Story, Part 3 June 18, 1983: After extensive training on the ground, Sally Ride became the first American woman to go into space. Her role on the Challenger was mission specialist, and she operated the shuttle's robotic arm to launch and retrieve communication satellites for Indonesia and Canada.

What do you think were the keys to Sally Ride's success? Write down 2 or 3 ideas.

Point out today's key school and team events.

Acknowledgments

One-Sentence Sharing In their table group, students take turns introducing themselves and sharing one sentence about one of their ideas from the announcements prompt. Repeat for one more round and then encourage groups to have a more free-flowing discussion. Listen in on each group and note four common keys to success to use in the Carousel activity.

Activity

Carousel Write one key to success on each of four pieces of chart paper, and post them around the room. In small groups, students rotate to each chart, brainstorm how that key might help them reach their goals, and list their ideas on the chart. Signal when it's time for groups to rotate to the next chart. Discuss the charts as a whole group as time allows.

Reflection "What would be the first idea you might try, and why?"

DAY 4 ■ Need Inspiration for Your Goals?

Arrival Welcome

Greet each student by name as they enter.

Announcements

> Dear Teammates,
>
> Along the path to achieving our goals, we are helped and encouraged by those who inspire us.
>
> **Sally's Story, Part 4** Sally Ride credits her high school science teacher with helping her pursue a career in science. After leaving NASA, Sally founded her own company, whose mission was to inspire young women to pursue careers in science, math, and technology.
>
> Who inspires you to reach your goals? Be ready to share.

Point out today's (and/or this weekend's) key school and team events.

Acknowledgments

One-Minute Brainstorm Students greet their tablemates by name and designate one group member as recorder. They spend one minute listing names of people who inspire them to reach their goals (for example, family members, teachers, and public figures). Then the first group reads their names aloud while you or a student volunteer list them on chart paper or a whiteboard. Recorders in other groups cross off any read-aloud names that also appear on their lists. Continue until all groups have read their list.

Activity

Just Like Me Use what you heard from table groups as prompts. Students who feel the statement applies to them stand up (or raise hands if standing is difficult) and say "Just like me" at the same time. Take time to observe who does not stand up (or doesn't stand up as often), and check in with them to hear their ideas. Repeat for as many rounds as time allows.

Reflection "How can you use a story like Sally Ride's to inspire you to keep reaching for your goals?"

Just Like Me Prompt Ideas

→ When teachers encourage me, I feel more confident in going for my goals.

→ I tell myself, "You can do it," to help me stay positive.

→ My friends inspire me because they're always there for me.

Rebooting Study Skills

Plan new strategies and academic behaviors for tackling tests and assignments

---

Skills Practiced This Week

Active listening

Organization

Perseverance

Study skills

Test-taking skills

Time management

DAY 1 ■ Getting Organized for Success

Arrival Welcome

Greet each student by name as they enter. Remind students to read the announcements message.

Announcements

Welcome, Hardworking Students!

This week you'll create success plans to become more efficient, independent students—starting with being organized for success.

Take a My Success Plan, and think about this question: Do you consider yourself to be an organized student? If so, what makes you organized? If not, what is hard for you about being organized?

Include upcoming school and team events in your messages this week.

Acknowledgments

Partner Chat At tables, students greet each other by name, then partner up to chat about the announcements prompt. Call on student volunteers to share one of their ideas with the whole group. As a way to invite students to share about a challenge they have, begin by sharing one of your own.

Activity

My Success Plan—Step 1 In their table group, students brainstorm strategies and skills for being better organized in four areas: Time Management, Study Skills, Homework, and Test Taking. Then they exchange ideas with a neighboring table group. Call on each group to share two or three ideas for each area and list these on chart paper or a whiteboard. Then have students complete Step 1 of their My Success Plan.* Collect everyone's plans. Students will use them for Day 2 and Day 3 this week.

Reflection "What are some benefits of being organized? Which organizational skills do you think are your strengths, and why? Which ones do you want to improve, and why?"

*A My Success Plan template is available to download; see page 19.

Strengthening Study Skills

Arrival Welcome

Greet each student by name as they enter.

Announcements

> Hello, Advisory Team,
>
> Yesterday you talked about how to become better organized.
>
> Today you'll continue with your success plan. You're going to talk about how to study for tests and quizzes, and how to complete homework and other assignments.
>
> Get your My Success Plan from yesterday. Think about the strategies you use to study and complete homework. Be ready to share.

Point out today's key school and team events.

Acknowledgments

What's Your Strategy? One student in each table group begins by greeting the student to their left with "Good morning, Willow. What's your strategy?" The student greeted responds with one strategy: "Good morning, Sasha. One strategy I use to study for tests is to review my class notes and completed quizzes." Continue around the table until everyone has shared two or three strategies. Display or hand out the Study Strategies sheet.* As a whole group, compare it with students' ideas.

Activity

Maître d' Call out a table grouping (for example: "Table for 3!") Students form standing table groups to discuss their responses to situations you pose (see examples in margin). Repeat as time allows, continuing to vary the table size.

Reflection Have students complete Step 2 of their My Success Plan handout. Ask: "Does your strategy for studying ever change based on the type of quiz/test or assignment?" Collect everyone's plans. Students will use them for Day 3.

*A Study Strategies sheet is available to download; see page 19.

Maître d' Examples

→ **Table for 2:** Your teacher said you might get a surprise quiz this week. What do you do to stay ready for it?

→ **Table for 4:** You have a paper due tomorrow. You have written an outline and the introductory paragraph. How can you complete the paper on time and get a decent grade on it?

→ **Table for 3:** You and two other classmates have to give a presentation next week. You can only meet in person once before the due date. What's your plan for giving a great presentation?

Rebooting Study Skills

Plan new strategies and academic behaviors for tackling tests and assignments

DAY 3 ▪ Strengthening Test-Taking Skills

Arrival Welcome

Greet each student by name as they enter. Encourage students to do a quick binder check as they get settled (see page 17).

Announcements

Dear Deep Thinkers,

Over the last 2 days, you have spent time building a plan for success. Today is the final piece of that plan: test-taking skills!

Get your My Success Plan handout. Think about how you take tests and quizzes. What strategies do you use to help you do well on these?

Point out today's key school and team events.

Acknowledgments

Partner Chat Students pair up with another table group member. After greeting their partner by name, they take turns sharing their responses to the announcements prompt. Encourage them to expand on their discussion: "If you struggle with a certain type of test—essay, for example—talk about why and then try to think up some helpful strategies together." You may also want to display or share the Test-Taking Tips* to support students' discussions.

Activity

Hand Up, Pair Up Round 1: Students find a partner from another table group, give a high five, and share one way they're working to become more organized. Round 2: Students find a partner from another table group, give a high five, and share one new strategy for studying that they are going to try. Rounds 3 and 4: Students find a partner from another table group, give a high five, and share their ideas for how they can do well on quizzes and tests.

Reflection Have students complete Step 3 of their My Success Plan.* Ask: "How does sharing strategies with each other help you create a new strategy plan?"

*Test-Taking Tips and My Success Plan templates are available to download; see page 19.

DAY 4 ■ Reaching Top Achievement

Arrival Welcome

Greet each student by name as they enter. Consider also giving a high five.

Announcements

> Hey, Active Achievers!
>
> To achieve any kind of goal, you need to make your best effort and keep a can-do attitude!
>
> **Quote of the Day** "Every mountaintop is within reach if you just keep climbing." —BARRY FINLAY, AUTHOR, PHILANTHROPIST
>
> Think about this quote and how you can apply it to your life.

Point out today's (and/or this weekend's) key school and team events.

Acknowledgments

Around-the-Table Talk At tables, students greet each other by name with a friendly "Good morning!" Then they take turns sharing their responses to the announcements prompt. Next, they share one thing they do that helps them achieve goals in all areas of their life (for example, eat healthy food).

Activity

Achieve-a-thon Tell students that instead of raising money in a phone-a-thon, they will "raise" tips for how to achieve goals. Working in pairs, students brainstorm tips in four categories—mental, emotional, social, and physical—and write down as many tips as possible within the time limit you set. When time is up, count the total number of tips for the whole group, read a few aloud, and display everyone's ideas for future use.

Reflection "Take a look at all the achievement tips you came up with. Which tips do you think will help you keep climbing to reach the goals you want to achieve?"

Goals, Take 3

Visualize new goals; identify personal strengths and stressors in pursuit of new goals

Skills Practiced This Week

Goal-setting
Managing stress
Self-confidence
Self-motivation
Visualization

NOTE Students will reference their SMART goal sheets from the "Setting New Goals" Advisory week on pages 66–69.

DAY 1 ■ Focal Point

Arrival Welcome

Greet each student by name as they enter. Remind students to read the announcements message.

Announcements

Welcome, Goal Setters,

Now that we're in the 3rd quarter, you've had good practice with setting and reaching your goals. This week you're going to focus on your strengths and how they can help you reach new goals over the next 8 weeks.

Quote of the Day "Your goals, minus your doubts, equal your reality."
—RALPH MARSTON, WRITER

Review your SMART goal sheet. Then write down 3 to 5 of your strengths on a sticky note. Be ready to share.

Include upcoming school and team events in your messages this week.

Acknowledgments

Mix and Mingle Students walk around the room, greeting each other by name and offering a handshake or some other friendly gesture. Then they share a strength from their list. After greeting at least five classmates, students return to their table group.

Activity

In the Bag Students imagine that they have an infinitely expandable bag. As a whole group, students brainstorm stressors or worries they have about achieving their goals. List these on chart paper or a whiteboard. Then have students close their eyes and imagine compressing their stressors or worries into one or more balls. On your signal, students visualize tossing the balls into their bag and then throwing the bag away.

Reflection "Think about today's quote. How do you think 'throwing away' your stressors and worries will help you focus on achieving your goals? What does achieving a goal look, sound, and feel like?"

You've Got the Power

Arrival Welcome

Greet each student by name as they enter. Consider adding in a handshake or a high five.

Announcements

> Hi, Aspiring Achievers!
>
> You've got the power to achieve your goals.
>
> **Quote of the Day** "I don't focus on what I'm up against. I focus on my goals and I try to ignore the rest." —VENUS WILLIAMS, PRO TENNIS PLAYER
>
> Rate your previous quarter experience on a scale of 1 to 4 (1—ugh; 2—just OK; 3—very good; 4—great!). Be ready to share your rating and why you chose it.

Point out today's key school and team events.

NOTE If students give their previous quarter a 1 or 2, be prepared to talk about why they gave this rating, and then help them establish a strategic plan to have a better new quarter, including asking others for help when needed.

Acknowledgments

Rating Our Previous Quarter Students pair up with a tablemate, greet their partner by name, and share their response to the announcements prompt. Then each table group figures out their group's average rating and lists that rating on a chart or whiteboard so that the whole group can figure out the whole-group average.

Activity

Picture This Have students close their eyes and take a deep breath. Guide them through this visualization: "Think about one goal you have for this quarter. Imagine yourself achieving this goal. What do you see? … What do you hear? … What do you feel? … What do you celebrate? … On three, open your eyes. One, two, three." Then have students mix and mingle, randomly pairing up and taking turns sharing their goal and one step they can take to achieve it.

Reflection "How does visualizing goal achievement lead to success? How might your strengths from yesterday also help you meet those goals?"

Goals, Take 3

Visualize new goals; identify personal strengths and stressors in pursuit of new goals

---

DAY 3 ■ Solid Goal

Arrival Welcome

Greet each student by name as they enter. Encourage students to do a quick binder check as they get settled (see page 17).

Announcements

> Hello, SMART Goalers!
>
> Knowing your strengths and visualizing success is half the journey. Now it's time to put your ideas into action.
>
> Pick up a new SMART goal sheet. Think about what goals you want to achieve this quarter and how your strengths can be used to achieve them.

Point out today's key school and team events.

Acknowledgments

Around-the-Table Sharing Students greet each of their tablemates by name and take turns sharing something new from their personal lives. Then they share one of their ideas from the announcements prompt.

Activity

Part 1: Creating a SMART Goal Plan Guide students, working individually or in pairs, in filling out their new SMART goal sheets.* Collect everyone's SMART goal sheets. Students will use these tomorrow.

Part 2: Do What I Said, Not What I Say Everyone stands at their desks. Call out an action one by one (see directions in margin). Students must follow the previously given action, not the current one.

Reflection "How does active listening and following instructions help you achieve your goals? How might you fix any mistakes or setbacks along the way to make sure you stay on track to achieving your goals?"

*A SMART goal template is available to download; see page 19.

Do What I Said, Not What I Say Directions

"Stand on one foot." (students do nothing)

"Hop on one foot." (students stand on one foot)

"Flap your arms." (students hop on one foot)

"Pat your head." (students flap their arms)

"Sit down." (students pat their heads)

"Fold your hands on your desks." (students sit down)

"Fold your hands on your desks." (students fold their hands on their desks)

DAY 4 ■ The Extra Mile

Arrival Welcome

Greet each student by name as they enter.

Announcements

> Hi, Advisory Team!
>
> You've learned a lot about your strengths and goals this week. Today you'll mark some milestones (actions or events) that will help you reach your goal.
>
> Get your SMART goal sheet from yesterday and review it. Think about key milestones that will help you achieve your goal(s). For example: If your goal is "perform at a piano recital," a milestone might be rehearsing your piece in front of family and friends.

Point out today's (and/or this weekend's) key school and team events.

Acknowledgments

Around-the-Table Chat Students greet each of their tablemates by name and take turns naming one SMART goal and one or two milestones. Then they have a more free-flowing discussion about how these milestones can help them stay on track to reach their goals.

Activity

Part 1: SMART Goal Milestones At tables, students use their SMART goal sheet to fill out their SMART Goal Milestones* sheet. Students can help each other brainstorm milestone steps for their SMART goal(s).

Part 2: Zoom Students begin seated. One student starts by looking at an immediate neighbor (to the left or right, in front or in back of them), saying "Zoom!" and then standing up. The student who receives the "Zoom!" quickly passes it to a seated neighbor and stands up. This continues around the room until it reaches the last seated student, who passes the "Zoom!" back to the leader and stands up. If time allows, pass the "Zoom!" around again until everyone is seated.

Reflection "How confident are you about reaching your goals now? What else can you do to make sure you reach them?"

*A SMART Goal Milestones template is available to download; see page 19.

Goals Wrap-Up

Map out a plan for reaching year-end goals

Skills Practiced This Week

Evaluating
Goal-setting
Perseverance
Self-motivation

NOTE If students give their previous quarter a 1 or 2, be prepared to talk about why they gave this rating, and then help them establish a strategic plan to have a better new quarter, including asking others for help when needed.

DAY 1 ■ Third Time's a Charm

Arrival Welcome

Greet each student by name as they enter. Remind students to read the announcements message.

Announcements

Welcome, Goal Keepers!

You've made it to our final quarter of the year. Do you know what that means? Time to set new goals!

Quote of the Day "Stay focused, go after your dreams, and keep moving toward your goals." —LL COOL J, RAPPER, ACTOR, ENTREPRENEUR

Think about all the goals you've set this year. What are some successes and challenges that stand out to you? Why? Be ready to share with a partner.

Include upcoming school and team events in your messages this week.

Acknowledgments

Inside-Outside Circles Students count off by twos. Ones form an inner circle and face out; twos form an outer circle and face in to form pairs. Partners greet each other by name and share one success and why it stands out. Twos then move one person to their right, greet their new partner, and share one challenge and why it stands out. Continue rounds as time allows, alternating between sharing a success and a challenge.

Activity

Rating Our Previous Quarter On their own, students rate their previous quarter experience on a scale of 1 to 4 (1—ugh; 2—just OK; 3—very good; 4—great!). Students pair up with a tablemate and share their rating and one reason why they chose it. Then each table group figures out their group's average rating and lists that rating on a chart or whiteboard so that the whole group can figure out the whole-group average.

Reflection Students write an anonymous response to this question on a piece of paper: "What is one goal you'd like to accomplish this quarter?" They crumple their paper into a "snowball" and toss it into the middle of the room. Then they pick up a nearby snowball and take turns reading the responses aloud.

DAY 2 ■ Adjusting Your Sails

Arrival Welcome

Greet each student by name as they enter. Consider adding in a handshake.

Announcements

> Ahoy, Smooth Sailors!
>
> **Quote of the Day** "I can't change the direction of the wind, but I can adjust my sails to always reach my destination." —JIMMY DEAN, SINGER, ACTOR, ENTREPRENEUR
>
> Think back on your goals from last quarter. (1) Do you want to revise them and/or make new ones? (2) How do you plan to reach your goals this quarter?

Point out today's key school and team events.

Acknowledgments

Interview Partner At tables, students pair up, greet their partner by name, and ask each other about their response to question #1 from the announcements prompt. Then pairs ask each other about their response to question #2.

Activity

Part 1: Creating a SMART Goal Plan Guide students, working individually or in pairs, in filling out their SMART goal sheets.* Collect everyone's SMART goal sheets. Students will use these tomorrow.

Part 2: Ma Zinga Standing in a circle, students point their arms straight into the center of the circle. Choose one student to be the leader, or ask for a volunteer. The group says, "Maaa . . ." with the "ah" sound gradually rising as students shake their fingers, hands, and arms to build up energy and a sense of team spirit. At the leader's signal—a nod of the head— the group quickly pulls back their hands while forming fists and cheers "Zinga!" loudly together. This motion pulls all that great team spirit and energy back into each individual.

Reflection "How might you 'adjust your sails' to meet your goals this quarter? Think of the milestones you'll need to achieve along the way in order to reach your goals. You'll be working on these tomorrow."

*A SMART goal template is available to download; see page 19.

Goals Wrap-Up

Map out a plan for reaching year-end goals

___

Number Freeze Directions

Set a timer for 60 seconds and say "Go!" Students try to get the target number of people to stand at the same time, following these rules: No one may talk or point; anyone may stand at any time, but no one may stand for more than 5 seconds at a time (students count to 5 silently). When you think the target number has been reached (or when the timer goes off), say "Freeze!" Students stay in position while you count those standing to see if the numbers match. Repeat with a new number.

DAY 3 ▪ One Step at a Time

Arrival Welcome

Greet each student by name as they enter. Encourage students to do a quick binder check as they get settled (see page 17).

Announcements

> Hello, Goal Getters!
>
> Today you're going to map out the course to reach your destination—achieving your goals this quarter.
>
> Get your SMART goal sheet from yesterday and review it. Think about key milestones that will help you achieve your goal. For example: If your SMART goal is "make a self-moving car for science class," a milestone might be assembling all the necessary supplies.

Point out today's key school and team events.

Acknowledgments

Around-the-Table Chat Students greet each of their tablemates by name and take turns naming one SMART goal and one or two milestones. Then they have a more free-flowing discussion about how these milestones can help them stay on track to reach their goals.

Activity

Part 1: SMART Goal Milestones Students stay with their table group and use their SMART goal sheets from yesterday to fill out their SMART Goal Milestones* sheet. Students can help each other brainstorm milestone steps for their SMART goals.

Part 2: Number Freeze Everyone begins sitting. Call out a target number—less than the total number of students but more than one-third the number. (For example, if there are 17 students present, pick a number between 6 and 16.) Continue with the directions at left.

Reflection "What are some similarities between Number Freeze and your goals and their key milestones?"

*A SMART Goal Milestones template is available to download; see page 19.

The Bigger Picture

Arrival Welcome

Greet each student by name as they enter.

Announcements

> Hello, Dreamers!
>
> You've been setting and accomplishing goals all year long. Today you'll think about how those goals connect to your long-term goals.
>
> **Quote of the Day** "Let us make our future now, and let us make our dreams tomorrow's reality." —MALALA YOUSAFZAI, ACTIVIST, NOBEL PRIZE LAUREATE
>
> What is one thing you dream to accomplish in the future? How might your goals today help you reach that dream (long-term goal)? Be ready to share with the whole group.

Point out today's (and/or this weekend's) key school and team events.

TIP Meeting One-on-One With Your Advisees

You can use this time to pair up with one advisee to get to know them better and continue to strengthen your relationship with them.

Acknowledgments

Hand Up, Pair Up Students find a partner from a different table group, give a high five, and share what the Quote of the Day means to them. Repeat for one or two more rounds.

Activity

Ball Toss Use any kind of squishy ball or beach ball. Students stand at their desks or in a circle. Ask question #1 from the announcements prompt and toss the ball to a student. That student shares their long-term goal, tosses the ball to someone else, and sits down. Continue until everyone has had a chance to respond, then do another round with students responding to question #2.

Reflection "Looking back on this week, list three big ideas that will help you reach your fourth-quarter goals, two questions you have about key milestones, and one takeaway or practical tip about your long-term goal that you plan to put into action."

Strengthen Advisor-Advisee Relationships

4-Day Plans

Tips for Strengthening Advisor-Advisee Relationships

All Grades

Advisory allows you to foster a growth mindset and make room for students to gain a more in-depth understanding of the word "trust." It allows students not to just say the word but to explore how it plays a part in everyday life, from home to school.

Advisory offers teachers and students the opportunity to work together in a positive and respectful way. Not only is it an excellent forum for building community, but it can also provide a safe space to address new or lingering conflicts. Guiding students through a respectful conflict-resolution process will help you further strengthen your Advisory community and improve your relationships with students.

Throughout Advisory, build your relationships with students by taking time to notice everyone's contributions, including those who are playing more supporting roles.

Grade Six

Students need room for their growing independence to bloom, but they also need to know they have your support. They're often less sure of themselves than they sound. Give them space to make their own choices, but let them know you're there for them when they need you.

Sixth graders may get defensive about mistakes, and they are more interested in learning new things than in "fixing" old work. Give them room to save face, and keep encouragement gentle when talking about revisions. Responding in writing is a good way to give them space to take in your comments.

At this stage, students may have trouble making decisions, but they're interested in learning about older and younger people. Sharing stories about your life and decisions may help them forge their own path.

Grade Seven

Seventh graders need a range of trusted adults in their lives to listen to and advise them, and enjoy talking to adults in a friendly and confident manner. As they are also excited by bigger assignments and projects, encourage them to identify or create student clubs, and to consider acting as a mentor.

With a growing interest in fairness, students will appreciate opportunities to discuss and modify rules and routines in a setting with clear, calm, and consistent adult authority. Listening and responding to their suggestions will go a long way in building their trust in you.

Students are growing more able to think abstractly about complex moral issues, and will take advice from teachers they trust. Let them know you take them seriously, and model positive ways to approach conflicts and other challenging situations.

Grade Eight

Eighth graders are often sensitive and may hold back from academic challenges in an effort to protect themselves. One of the things they need most is acknowledgement as individuals, so support them by carefully watching and listening to them and gently encouraging them to take risks in the classroom.

Time spent with friends is crucial, but students also tend to spend a lot of time alone. Suggest participation in extracurricular activities, service projects, or tutoring younger children in order to help students build important cognitive and SEL skills.

Despite eighth graders' sensitivity, they also exhibit high energy and a good sense of humor. They tend to challenge authority figures as they establish their own personalities. Maintaining your own sense of humor will help you and your students have a posi-

Admiration Nation

Form a stronger Advisory community through the sharing of values and discovery of commonalities

Skills Practiced This Week

Building community
Empathy
Problem-solving
Self-confidence
Self-reflection

DAY 1 ■ Who Do You CLAIM to Be?

Arrival Welcome

Greet each student by name as they enter. Remind students to read the announcements message.

Announcements

> Welcome Back to Advisory!
>
> Since our Advisory meetings have started, we've spent time getting to know each other. But there's so much more to learn!
>
> On an index card, write 3 facts about yourself: 1—Something that's true for most students (I go to _____ Middle School); 2—Something that's true only for some students (I take part in an extracurricular activity); 3—Something that is most likely true for just you (I have a brother named Clive).

Include upcoming school and team events in your messages this week.

Acknowledgments

Mix and Mingle Students walk around the room, greet each other by name, and share one word that describes who they are. (Consider joining in on this activity.) After students have talked with three to four classmates, ask a few volunteers to share some words they heard.

Activity

Shared Truths Collect the index cards and choose one. Tell students you're going to read the statements one at a time, and to pay attention to who stands and who sits after each statement. 1—If the first statement is true for students, they stand up. 2—If the second statement is true, they remain standing while other students sit down. 3—After the third statement is read, the only person standing should be the student who wrote the card. If more than one student is standing, the other student(s) can share how the statement is true for them as well. Repeat as time allows. Over the next few days, go through the rest of the cards until all have been read.

Reflection Gather everyone in a circle. Ask: "What surprised you today? Why?"

DAY 2 ■ Advice Columnist

Arrival Welcome

Greet each student by name as they enter. Consider adding in a handshake.

Announcements

Hello, Advisory Team!

Quote of the Day "My advice to you is to be true to yourself and everything else will be fine." —ELLEN DeGENERES, COMEDIAN, TELEVISION HOST

Is this quote true for you?

Think about the best advice you've ever received. Be ready to share.

Point out today's key school and team events.

Acknowledgments

Table Talk Students greet their tablemates by name with "Hola" ("Hello" in Spanish) and share their response to the announcements prompt. After all students have shared with their group, ask for a few volunteers to share their response with the whole group.

Activity

Advice Columnists With the whole group, brainstorm and list questions students want advice about ("How can I develop better study habits?" "How can I stay motivated in math class?"). Have students pair up with someone they don't usually sit or work with (include yourself). One student is the advice seeker; the other is the advice columnist. The seeker asks one of the questions from the brainstormed list (or their own question), and the columnist responds with how they would handle the situation. Then they switch roles and ask and respond to the same question. Repeat with a new question. To wrap up, each pair writes one question and the best advice for it, and posts it on an anchor chart for others to read.

Reflection Gather everyone in a circle. Ask: "How hard is it to give useful advice, and why? To receive advice? Why?"

Admiration Nation

Form a stronger Advisory community through the sharing of values and discovery of commonalities

DAY 3 ■ People We Admire, PART 1

Arrival Welcome

Greet each student by name as they enter. Encourage students to do a quick binder check as they get settled (see page 17).

Announcements

Dear Admirable People,

Do you know that I admire each and every one of you? (To admire means to hold in high regard.) You all work hard here in Advisory, and you're supportive of one another. These are very admirable qualities!

On a sticky note, list 3 people you admire—1 living, 1 deceased, and 1 fictional—and why you admire them.

Point out today's key school and team events.

Acknowledgments

Mix and Mingle Students walk around the room, greet each other by name, and share one person they admire and why (consider joining in). After students have talked with three to four classmates, ask a few volunteers to share a person they admire and why with the whole group. Then have everyone add their three people to a chart or whiteboard.

Activity

Word Splash In their table group, students create a Word Splash* about people they admire using words that represent why they admire them (students can also use pictures if they prefer). Then each group presents and explains their Word Splash to the whole group. Display the Word Splashes where everyone can see them.

Reflection "What are some similarities among all the people you admire? How do personal role models positively influence your life?"

*A Word Splash template and example are available to download; see page 19.

> **TIP**
> ### Meeting One-on-One With Your Advisees
> You can use this time to pair up with one advisee to get to know them better and continue to strengthen your relationship with them.

People We Admire, PART 2

Arrival Welcome

Greet each student by name as they enter.

Announcements

> Congratulations, Team!
>
> We've had an admirable time this week during Advisory. All of you helped make that possible—and that's great team spirit!
>
> List 3 more people you admire and why: someone in our community, an adult in our school, and a student in our school.

Point out today's (and/or this weekend's) key school and team events.

Acknowledgments

Around-the-Table Sharing Students greet each of their tablemates by name. Then they take turns sharing one of the people they listed in response to the announcements prompt, and one reason why they admire them. Ask a few volunteers to share some of the people their group talked about.

TIP If students can't think of people at school, or prefer not to share those names publicly, suggest they consider people they admire in their family or the wider community.

Activity

Snowball Explain that students should not write their names on their papers. Students write down on a piece of paper one person they admire and why (it can be anyone; it doesn't have to be someone they listed today or yesterday). Write down your response, too. Everyone crumples up their paper into a "snowball" and tosses it into the middle of the room. Everyone picks up a nearby snowball and takes turns reading the snowballs aloud. Collect all the snowballs.

Reflection Review the people students admire from yesterday and today. Ask: "The people we admire can inspire us. How are you inspired?"

Building Trust

Become personally invested in building trust through brainstorming, reflection, and creative activities

---

Skills Practiced This Week

Building positive relationships

Building trust

Creative thinking

Inferring/interpreting

Self-reflection

DAY 1 ▪ Trust 101

Arrival Welcome

Greet each student by name as they enter. Remind students to read the announcements message.

Announcements

> Welcome, Trustworthy Team!
>
> This week we will discuss how to build trust. Trust can be defined as having faith in a person's reliability, honesty, and dependability.
>
> Trust means . . .
>
> What does trust mean to you? Finish the above sentence on a sticky note. For example: "Trust means I can count on someone to be on time for a study group meet-up." Be ready to share.

Include upcoming school and team events in your messages this week.

Acknowledgments

One-Sentence Sharing In their table group, students greet each other by name and then take turns sharing a one-sentence response to the announcements prompt. Then they have a more free-flowing conversation about trust. Invite a few volunteers to share their "Trust means . . ." sentence with the whole group. (Consider sharing your sentence first.)

Activity

Scrambled Words With a Side of Toast Give each table group a phrase about trust to unscramble. For example: gnebi tnhose (being honest); teegnim no mtie (meeting on time); gkinas ofr phel (asking for help); a tnjoi ffrteo (a joint effort). Each group discusses the importance of their phrases with regard to trust and creates a quote (the "toast") about their phrase to inspire everyone in Advisory. Each group shares their phrase and quote with the whole group.

Reflection Gather everyone in a circle. Ask: "Why do you think it's important to have trust in your relationships with classmates? Teachers? Friends? Family?"

Arrival Welcome

Greet each student by name as they enter.

Announcements

> Hi, Resolute Students!
>
> Yesterday you came up with many great ideas about trust. Today you're going to dig deeper into what trust is all about.
>
> Think about this: How is trust like a house? (For example: Trust is like a house because it must have a solid foundation.)

Point out today's key school and team events.

Acknowledgments

Making Connections In their table group, students greet each other and then brainstorm possible connections between "house" and "trust," coming up with valid reasons to support their connections.

Activity

Amazing Analogies Write the following on chart paper or a whiteboard: "Trust is like a house because _____." Each group chooses one of their connections to create their own analogy similar to the example in the announcements prompt. Share your own analogy with the whole group first. Then have each table group take turns sharing their analogy. Post everyone's analogies.

Reflection "Which analogy do you have the strongest connection to, and why? How can these analogies help you build more trust with others in our school?"

Building Trust

Become personally invested in building trust through brainstorming, reflection, and creative activities

DAY 3 ■ Building Trust in Action

Arrival Welcome

Greet each student by name as they enter. Encourage students to do a quick binder check as they get settled (see page 17).

Announcements

Hello, Trust Builders!

Today we're going to connect our ideas to better build trust at our school.

What are some actions that demonstrate trustworthiness (for example, keeping language about others positive)? Be ready to share your ideas.

Point out today's key school and team events.

Acknowledgments

Group Brainstorm In their table group, students discuss their responses to the announcements prompt. Then they brainstorm which ideas are their top three actions that demonstrate trustworthiness (consider joining a group).

Activity

Part 1: Vote on It Each group shares their top three actions with the whole group; list these on chart paper or a whiteboard. Take a vote to find the top three to five actions and circle these.

Part 2: Building Trust in Action, Step 1 Students break into small groups and create a "Building Trust" script/poster/comic strip using one or more of the top voted actions. Collect everyone's script/poster/comic strip. Students will present these in tomorrow's Advisory.

Reflection "We all make mistakes. How might trust get broken? Think about how it can be rebuilt. We'll explore that more tomorrow."

Arrival Welcome

Greet each student by name as they enter. Consider also giving a high five.

Announcements

> Hello, Reliable Team!
>
> Today we're going to work together to put building trust into action.
>
> Get your "Building Trust" script/poster/comic strip. Then ponder this: When trust is broken, how can it be rebuilt? Be ready to share.

Point out today's (and/or this weekend's) key school and team events.

TIP

Meeting One-on-One With Your Advisees

You can use this time to pair up with one advisee to get to know them better and continue to strengthen your relationship with them.

Acknowledgments

Hand Up, Pair Up Students find a partner from a different table group, give a high five, and share their response to the announcements prompt. Repeat for one or two more rounds.

Activity

Building Trust in Action, Step 2 Small groups present their "Building Trust" script/poster/comic strip to the whole group. Invite students to share any similarities they noticed. If possible, have students present or display their "Building Trust" script/poster/comic strips for the greater school community.

Reflection "Looking back on this week, list three big ideas that you learned about trust, two questions that you have about trust, and one takeaway or practical tip about trust that you plan to put into action."

Student-Led Advisory Planning

Practice organization and cooperation by planning an Advisory meeting

Skills Practiced This Week

Cooperation
Leadership
Organization
Self-confidence
Strategizing

NOTE Students will share what they learned from the "Interviewing School Leaders" Advisory week on pages 118–121.

DAY 1 ▪ What Makes a Leader?

Arrival Welcome

Greet each student by name as they enter. Remind students to read the announcements message.

Announcements

> Welcome, Future Leaders!
>
> This week you're going to plan how to lead your own Advisory meeting. First, you're going to share what you learned from your interview with the school leader you admire.
>
> Think about (1) what leadership skills you admire about the school leader you interviewed, and why; (2) what you learned (2–3 things) about this leader during your interview. Be ready to share.

Include upcoming school and team events in your messages this week.

Acknowledgments

Around-the-Table Chat Going clockwise, students greet their tablemates by name and take turns answering question #1 of the announcements prompt. Going counterclockwise, students take turns answering question #2. Then they have a more free-flowing discussion about what skills their school leaders have in common. Invite a few volunteers to share one of their group's ideas.

Activity

Common Commonalities Individually, students list the leadership qualities that best represent their school leader. Then students share their list with their tablemates. The group circles any leadership qualities that all group members have listed or agreed upon, and a spokesperson from each group shares their commonalities with the whole group. List these, and save the list for students to reference the rest of the week.

Reflection "Look at all these qualities that make up the leaders you admire! How might these qualities help you as you plan and lead your Advisory?"

Choosing a Topic

Arrival Welcome

Greet each student by name as they enter.

Announcements

> Hi, Brainstormers!
>
> Advisory is made up of four components:
>
> 1) Arrival welcome—a greeting at the door
>
> 2) Announcements—an interactive message, like this one
>
> 3) Acknowledgments—a sharing of responses to the announcements
>
> 4) Activity—a whole-group activity
>
> Following the activity, a question or topic is posed that prompts student reflection on the day's meeting.
>
> Each Advisory has a topic (for example: family histories; bullying prevention). What topic would you like for your Advisory? Be ready to share.

Point out today's key school and team events.

Acknowledgments

Mix and Mingle Students walk around the room, greeting each other by name and offering a handshake or another friendly gesture. Then they exchange their ideas from the announcements prompt. After students have talked with three to four classmates, ask a few volunteers to share their topic idea with the whole group.

Activity

Consensus Mapping (variation) Divide students into four groups and give each group chart paper. Assign a recorder, who draws a circle in the middle of the paper and labels it "Consensus." Each student lists their Advisory ideas on a separate piece of paper and circles their top three ideas. They then take turns nominating one of their circled ideas for consensus. See next steps at left.

Reflection "What made reaching consensus successful? Did you encounter any hurdles? If so, how did you leap over them to come to agreement?"

TIP

Meeting One-on-One With Your Advisees

You can use this time to pair up with one advisee to get to know them better and continue to strengthen your relationship with them.

Consensus Mapping Directions

If all members agree, the recorder lists the idea on the chart paper (but not in the circle). The group then reaches consensus on their top three ideas. The recorder lists these in the consensus circle. Post the consensus maps and leave them up for the rest of this week's Advisory.

Student-Led Advisory Planning

Practice organization and cooperation by planning an Advisory meeting

DAY 3 ■ Planning Advisory, PART 1

Arrival Welcome

Greet each student by name as they enter. Encourage students to do a quick binder check as they get settled (see page 17).

Announcements

> Hello, Advisory Planners!
>
> Today and tomorrow you're going to plan your group's Advisory day! But first, you must finalize your topic.
>
> Review everyone's Consensus Map. Star your number one topic choice in each group's consensus circle (including your own). Then join your group from yesterday.

Point out today's key school and team events.

Acknowledgments

Swap Meet Each group tallies up the stars on their Consensus Map. The topic with the most stars will be the group's Advisory topic (for example: family histories). On their own, students write down ideas about that topic that they'd like to include in their Advisory (for example: family customs; places families come from). Then they swap ideas with their groupmates.

Activity

NOTE Collect everyone's Advisory Plans for students to use tomorrow, and make copies of Advisory plans from this book that have the same acknowledgments format and activities each group chose.

Planning Advisory, Part 1 Hand each group an Advisory Plan template* and an Advisory Acknowledgments and Activity List.* From the ideas generated during Swap Meet, each group chooses one or two ideas they want to include in their Advisory. Together, they write their announcements message on their Advisory Plan. Then they choose and write down an acknowledgments format and activity title from the list and share these with the whole group.

Reflection Gather everyone in a circle. Ask: "How did knowing your topic help with planning your Advisory?"

*The Advisory Plan template and the Advisory Acknowledgments and Activity List are available to download; see page 19.

DAY 4 ■ Planning Advisory, PART 2

Arrival Welcome

Greet each student by name as they enter. Consider also giving a handshake.

Announcements

> Congrats, Advisory Team!
>
> With just a little more planning, you'll be ready to lead Advisory. How exciting! I look forward to participating next week!
>
> Review the common leadership qualities you listed at the beginning of this week. What leadership qualities have you noticed while your group planned your Advisory day? Share with a partner from your group.

Point out today's (and/or this weekend's) key school and team events.

Acknowledgments

Group Brainstorm Hand each group their Advisory Plan template and a sample Advisory plan from this book with the same acknowledgments format they chose. Students brainstorm how to adapt the acknowledgements to fit their group's Advisory topic, and then write their own. Guide students in writing as needed.

Activity

Planning Advisory, Part 2 Hand each group a sample Advisory plan from this book that has the same activity they chose. Students brainstorm how to adapt the activity to fit their Advisory topic and then write their own. Review each group's acknowledgments and activity, and help them make any changes as needed. Finally, have each group create a reflection question for the whole group to think about at the end of their Advisory.

Reflection Gather everyone in a circle. Ask: "What's one thing that surprised you during this week's Advisory planning?"

NOTE
Collect everyone's completed Advisory plan for use in the "Student-Led Advisory Week" on pages 96–99.

Assign each group a day that they will lead Advisory (Group 1 will lead the first day, Group 2 the second day, and so on).

Student-Led Advisory Week

Exercise leadership and independence by running an Advisory meeting

---

Skills Practiced This Week

Leadership

Organization

Public speaking

Responsibility

Teamwork

> **NOTE** Each day this week, one group will present the Advisory meeting that they planned during the "Student-Led Advisory Planning" Advisory week on pages 92–95.
>
> After each group presents, collect their Advisory plan to use during their debrief in the "Teamwork and Team Spirit" Advisory week on pages 158–161.

DAY 1 ▪ Student Advisory Leaders, GROUP 1

Arrival Welcome

Tips for Advisor

➡ Before students enter the classroom, post the announcements message Group 1 wrote.

➡ Greet each student by name as they enter. Remind Groups 2, 3, and 4 which day they are leading Advisory this week (assigned on Day 4 of "Student-Led Advisory Planning" Advisory week; see page 95).

➡ If time allows, have Group 1 greet each student by name as they enter the classroom and give a friendly handshake, fist bump, or high five.

➡ Remind students to read the announcements message.

➡ Hand Group 1 their Advisory plan.

Announcements

Tips for Advisor

➡ Point out upcoming school and team events.

➡ Inform Group 1 you are available to help if they need guidance, but your main role this week is Student.

➡ Respond to the announcements prompt, and participate in today's Advisory as a student. Hold back any "teaching" feedback during Advisory.

Acknowledgments

Tips for Advisor

➡ Join in on the acknowledgments.

➡ Give student leaders a 1-minute warning to signal wrap-up if necessary.

Activity

Tips for Advisor

➡ Join in on the activity.

➡ Give student leaders a 1-minute warning to signal wrap-up if necessary.

Reflection Tip for Advisor After the whole group responds to Group 1's reflection question, tell students that they will all have the chance to reflect on their Advisory day at the end of the week.

Student Advisory Leaders, ## GROUP 2

Arrival Welcome

Tips for Advisor

➡ Before students enter, post the announcements message Group 2 wrote.

➡ Greet each student by name as they enter. Remind Groups 3 and 4 which day they are leading Advisory.

➡ If time allows, have Group 2 greet each student by name as they enter the classroom and give a friendly handshake, fist bump, or high five.

➡ Remind students to read the announcements message.

➡ Hand Group 2 their Advisory plan.

Announcements

Tips for Advisor

➡ Point out today's key school and team events.

➡ Inform Group 2 you are available to help if they need guidance, but your main role this week is Student.

➡ Respond to the announcements prompt, and participate in today's Advisory as a student. Hold back any "teaching" feedback during Advisory.

Acknowledgments

Tips for Advisor

➡ Join in on the acknowledgments.

➡ Give student leaders a 1-minute warning to signal wrap-up if necessary.

Activity

Tips for Advisor

➡ Join in on the activity.

➡ Give student leaders a 1-minute warning to signal wrap-up if necessary.

R̲B̲ eflection Tip for Advisor After the whole group responds to Group 2's reflection question, tell students that they will all have the chance to reflect on their Advisory day at the end of the week.

Student-Led Advisory Week

Exercise leadership and independence by running an Advisory meeting

DAY 3 ■ # Student Advisory Leaders,
GROUP 3

Arrival Welcome

Tips for Advisor

➡ Before students enter, post the announcements message Group 3 wrote.

➡ Greet each student by name as they enter. Remind Group 4 which day they are leading Advisory.

➡ If time allows, have Group 3 greet each student by name as they enter the classroom and give a friendly handshake, fist bump, or high five.

➡ Remind students to read the announcements message.

➡ Hand Group 3 their Advisory plan.

Announcements

Tips for Advisor

➡ Point out today's key school and team events.

➡ Inform Group 3 you are available to help if they need guidance, but your main role this week is Student.

➡ Respond to the announcements prompt, and participate in today's Advisory as a student. Hold back any "teaching" feedback during Advisory.

Acknowledgments

Tips for Advisor

➡ Join in on the acknowledgments.

➡ Give student leaders a 1-minute warning to signal wrap-up if necessary.

Activity

Tips for Advisor

➡ Join in on the activity.

➡ Give student leaders a 1-minute warning to signal wrap-up if necessary.

Reflection Tip for Advisor After the whole group responds to Group 3's reflection question, tell students that they will all have the chance to reflect on their Advisory day at the end of the week.

Student Advisory Leaders,
GROUP 4

Arrival Welcome

Tips for Advisor

➡ Before students enter, post the announcements message Group 4 wrote.

➡ Greet each student by name as they enter.

➡ If time allows, have Group 4 greet each student by name as they enter the classroom and give a friendly handshake, fist bump, or high five.

➡ Remind students to read the announcements message.

➡ Hand Group 4 their Advisory plan.

Announcements

Tips for Advisor

➡ Point out today's (and/or this weekend's) key school and team events.

➡ Inform Group 4 you are available to help if they need guidance, but your main role this week is Student.

➡ Respond to the announcements prompt, and participate in today's Advisory as a student. Hold back any "teaching" feedback during Advisory.

Acknowledgments

Tips for Advisor

➡ Join in on the acknowledgments.

➡ Give student leaders a 1-minute warning to signal wrap-up if necessary.

Activity

Tips for Advisor

➡ Join in on the activity.

➡ Give student leaders a 1-minute warning to signal wrap-up if necessary.

Reflection Tip for Advisor After the whole group responds to Group 4's reflection question, hold a celebratory whole-week Ma Zinga reflection (see directions at left).

Ma Zinga Reflection

Standing in a circle, students take turns naming one thing they liked best about planning their Advisory day. After everyone has shared, students point their arms straight into the center of the circle. Choose one student to be the leader, or ask for a volunteer. The group says "Maaa . . ." with the "ah" sound gradually rising as students shake their fingers, hands, and arms to build up energy and a sense of team spirit. At the leader's signal—a nod of the head—the group quickly pulls back their hands while forming fists and cheers "Zinga!" loudly together. This motion pulls all that great team spirit and energy back into each individual.

Develop Communication and Social Skills

4-Day Plans

Tips for Developing Communication and Social Skills

All Grades

It takes time for middle school students to become effective communicators. Having patience and coaching them will help them develop these essential skills.

As the school year progresses, students will begin to feel more comfortable and better able to practice negotiating difficult situations. Always stay mindful of those in the group who may be in the middle of a difficult social situation or disagreement with each other when scaffolding these activities.

Later in the year, younger middle schoolers will be feeling more confident in their place in the building, and seventh and eighth graders will already be old pros. All grades will enjoy opportunities for personal, student-driven interactions with adults in school.

Grade Six

Depending on the range of development in the group, you may be juggling impulsive, ever-ready-to-debate students with those who have more developed insight and empathy. Be strategic about forming student groups during activities.

Also be aware of students' tendency at this age to worry about who's "in" and who's "out." Stay mindful about issues of inclusion and exclusion as you group students for collaborative work. Sixth graders enjoy competition, particularly as a team, so build community through group activities and challenges that allow students to come together and beat their previous records.

Students may regularly question or challenge the adults in school, not always politely or respectfully. Avoid correcting them in front of their peers; find a private time and place to coach them to let them save face.

Grade Seven

Seventh graders are interested in building stronger, more positive social skills and communication skills in the context of being respectful, responsible team members. They also want to focus on how to be open-minded, less sensitive, and more resilient when encountering ideas that differ from theirs. Emphasize perspective-taking and collaboration during group discussions and activities.

Students are also more likely to take an interest in getting to know classmates they haven't been friends with before. Encourage these budding friendships by grouping students with classmates they don't work with often.

Support students in identifying adults in the building they can trust. This will help anchor and guide them as they think through serious social issues they face at home and school.

Grade Eight

Eighth graders may complain that they're bored or just want to be left alone. Encourage them to take positive risks like participating in class discussions or being the presenter for their group, and help them recognize their significance to the class.

Because of their sensitivity, eighth graders may need more support than older or younger students when working in groups. Often, students will work best with a single partner. They like to be able to choose their own partners or group members, but may need guidance from the teacher if social struggles are leading to a negative tone during partner or group work.

These students are very interested in social justice, though they may have difficulty translating that into their own social situations. Encourage thinking globally about local and personal difficulties.

The Art of Communication

Discover how kindness and respect lead to more meaningful communication

---

Skills Practiced This Week

Active listening

Building positive relationships

Speaking essentials

DAY 1 ▪ Artful Communication, PART 1

Arrival Welcome

Greet each student by name as they enter. Remind them to read the announcements message. Consider having quiet music playing in the background.

Announcements

Dear Cool Communicators,

This week, you'll be focusing on the art of communication. It's part of everything we do!

Quote of the Day "To effectively communicate, we must realize that we are all different in the way we perceive the world and use this understanding as a guide to our communication with others." —TONY ROBBINS, AUTHOR, ENTREPRENEUR

How important do you think communication is in school and in life? Exchange ideas with your table partner.

Include upcoming school and team events in your messages this week.

Acknowledgments

Table Talk Students greet their tablemates by name and take turns sharing a summary of their partner's responses to the announcements prompt. As a group, students brainstorm and list the qualities (patience, thoughtfulness) and skills (waiting to speak, speaking clearly) that are essential for effective communication. Have groups display or present their lists.

Activity

Info Exchange Each student gets an Info Exchange Question Card.* Give them some think time; then students find a partner and take turns reading their cards and sharing and discussing their responses. Encourage them to explain the thinking behind their responses. After a few minutes, students exchange cards and find new partners. Repeat as time allows. Ask for volunteers to share one highlight from their exchanges.

Reflection "What do you think are the most important qualities and skills for being an effective communicator?"

*An Info Exchange Question Card template is available to download; see page 19.

DAY 2 ■ Artful Communication, PART 2

Arrival Welcome

Greet each student by name as they enter. Encourage students to do a quick "re-org" of their backpack, notebooks, folders, and so on, as they get settled.

Announcements

Hello, Collaborative Communicators:

Today you're going to dig deeper into how we can all become better communicators.

Quote of the Day "Our cellphones can do everything, but they're bad at letting us talk to each other." —RAINBOW ROWELL, AUTHOR

Get a marker—make sure it's a dark color. Think about what it is exactly that makes communication work well.

Point out today's key school and team events.

Acknowledgments

Partner Interview In their table group, students pair up, greet their table partner by name, and take turns interviewing each other about (1) what the quote means to them; (2) what they think makes communication work well. Next students summarize what their partner said with their table group. Ask a few volunteers to share their group's ideas with the whole group.

Activity

Graffiti Headings

→ Listening Essentials

→ Speaking Essentials

→ Using Manners

→ Agreeing Thoughtfully

→ Disagreeing Respectfully

Graffiti Post chart paper with the headings shown at left. Students "graffiti" their ideas on the charts (starting at any chart, going in any order, writing in any style anywhere on the chart). Then they form small groups and find common themes and trends among the completed charts. Each group summarizes their findings for the whole group.

Reflection Gather everyone in a circle. Ask: "Based on our charts, what do you now think are the most important qualities and skills for being an effective communicator? What's one thing you will do this week to become a more effective communicator?"

The Art of Communication

Discover how kindness and respect lead to more meaningful communication

---

DAY 3 ■ # Kindness and Communication, PART 1

Arrival Welcome

Greet each student by name and with a warm smile as they enter.

Announcements

Greetings, Kind Communicators,

Yesterday you talked about the importance of communication. Today you're going to add another layer to that—kindness.

Quote of the Day "Courage. Kindness. Friendship. Character. These are the qualities that define us as human beings, and propel us, on occasion, to greatness." —FROM *WONDER* BY R. J. PALACIO

Read the quote again, and think about what it means to you.

Point out today's key school and team events.

Acknowledgments

One Thing The student whose birthday is closest to January 1 starts. That student turns to the student on their left, greets them by name, and asks: "What's one thing you remember from yesterday's Graffiti charts?" The student returns the greeting and shares their response. Repeat for several rounds.

Beat the Clock Prompts

➜ **1st prompt:** Define kindness in as many ways as you can.

➜ **2nd prompt:** List ways you show kindness to others.

➜ **3rd prompt:** List ways you would like others to be kind to you.

➜ **4th prompt:** List ways you can communicate kindness to others.

Activity

Beat the Clock In small groups, students have 60 seconds to brainstorm as many ideas as they can in response to each of four prompts (see prompts at left). Have each group choose a note-taker to record their ideas, and for each prompt, signal when to begin and end. After groups complete their brainstorming, they discuss and choose their top two ideas for each prompt (eight ideas in all). Each group then presents their ideas to the whole group. Record these on chart paper. Discuss common themes and trends.

Reflection Gather everyone in a circle. Ask: "Think about the work you did this week around communication. How does kindness connect to communication? What's something you can do to communicate more kindness to others?"

DAY 4 ▪ Kindness and Communication, PART 2

Arrival Welcome

Greet each student by name as they enter. Consider also giving a high five.

Announcements

Dear Complimenting Communicators,

Today is a great day to practice the art of communication and kindness. Here's a short passage from *Awaken* by Katie Kacvinsky to get us started:

> Justin: "Girls like compliments, don't they?"
>
> Madeline: "I think everyone does if it's sincere. Not just girls."

Think about the people at your table. What's one compliment you can give them (about their positive actions)?

Point out today's (and/or this weekend's) key school and team events.

Acknowledgments

Giving Compliments As a whole group, brainstorm compliments and list (or invite a student volunteer to list) them. At tables, students greet each other by name and offer a compliment. For example: "Good morning, Felix. Your kind words yesterday helped me have a great day." Emphasize that each compliment should be about the person's positive actions, not about their appearance.

Activity

Four Corners (variation) Post chart paper around the room with the questions shown at left (one question per chart). With their table group, students go to a corner and discuss the posted question. At the end of their discussion, they write their top three responses on the chart. Signal for groups to rotate to the next corner and repeat until groups have been to all four corners. Give groups time to review and discuss the completed charts.

Four Corners Questions

➡ How will you use what you learned about communication in school? At home?

➡ What did you learn about yourself this week?

➡ If you could teach other students communication skills, which would you teach?

➡ What communication skills should we work on as a whole group in Advisory?

Reflection Remind students that improving communication skills takes time and effort. Ask: "What are some ways everyone can work on improving communication skills here in Advisory?" Implement students' ideas in future Advisories.

Speaking Up

Experience how engaged, compassionate comunication strengthens community bonds

---

Skills Practiced This Week

Active listening

Assertiveness

Creative thinking

Building positive relationships

Speaking essentials

DAY 1 ■ Communication 101

Arrival Welcome

Greet each student by name as they enter. Remind students to read the announcements message.

Announcements

Welcome, Advisory Team!

You're going to delve into communication during our meetings this week.

Quote of the Day "Do the best you can until you know better. Then when you know better, do better." —MAYA ANGELOU, POET, AUTHOR

Think about what this quote means to you. Be prepared to share your thoughts with a partner.

Include upcoming school and team events in your messages this week.

Acknowledgments

Interview At tables, students pair up, greet their partner by name, and take turns interviewing each other about what the quote means to them. Students then take turns interviewing the other members of their table group about what this quote means in terms of improving their communication skills. Ask two or three volunteers to share their group's ideas with the whole group.

Activity

No Way Display a sentence that gives several details, such as who did what, when, where, and with whom. For example: "Last month, my friend James and I went to the park and played basketball, had ice cream, and listened to music." Students take turns changing just one element of the sentence until everyone has had a turn and the original sentence has changed completely. A recorder makes edits to the displayed sentence. Conclude by having everyone say: "Oh, yeah! *That's* what happened!"

Reflection Gather everyone in a circle. Ask: "What communication skills did you need to be successful with this activity? When can you use these skills to help everyone communicate better with each other?"

DAY 2 ■ Communication 102

Arrival Welcome

Greet each student by name as they enter. Consider having a song like "There for You" by Martin Garrix and Troye Sivan play in the background.

Announcements

Dear Effective Communicators,

Communication is like a glue that holds every relationship together.

Quote of the Day "Nothing lowers the level of conversation more than raising the voice." —STANLEY HOROWITZ, AUTHOR

On a sticky note, write 3 strategies you use to raise the level of communication and keep it positive.

Point out today's key school and team events.

Acknowledgments

What's Your Strategy? One student in each table group begins by greeting the student to their left with "Hi, _____. What's your strategy?" The student greeted responds, "Hi, _____. One strategy I use to keep my communication positive is [student names one of their strategies]." Continue around the table until everyone has shared. Display the sticky notes, and ask for volunteers to share an idea that was new to them.

Activity

NOTE Brainwriting is writing down ideas before sharing them aloud.

Encore Brainwriting Give small groups sticky notes and large paper; assign recorders. Recorders make a T-chart on the paper and write "talk/listen" in the left-hand column. Individually, students list songs that contain "talk" or "listen" on sticky notes (one song per sticky note) and post them under "talk/listen" on the T-chart. The group discusses personal connections to the songs. Recorders summarize their group's connections in the right-hand column. Display the finished charts.

Reflection Gather everyone in a circle. Ask: "Think about what it takes to improve your communication skills. What will you do to improve your skills? What can you do to help others improve theirs?"

Speaking Up

Experience how engaged, compassionate comunication strengthens community bonds

TIP Meeting One-on-One With Your Advisees

You can use this time to pair up with one advisee to get to know them better and continue to strengthen your relationship with them.

DAY 3 ▪ Positive Assertiveness 101

Arrival Welcome

Greet each student by name as they enter. Consider doing a quick check-in about how students are feeling by having them show a thumbs-up (great), thumbs-down (poor), or thumbs-sideways (so-so).

Announcements

Welcome Back, Team!

Yesterday you came up with some great communication strategies and skills. Today you're going to explore another key communication skill: speaking up for yourself or being assertive.

Pick up a Positive Assertiveness LSF chart. List what you think being assertive should look, sound, and feel like here at school with your peers. (If you're not sure what "assertive" means, check the dictionary!)

Point out today's key school and team events.

Acknowledgments

Partner Chat In their table group, students talk with a partner about their Positive Assertiveness LSF Chart.* Encourage students to record any of their partner's ideas that they connect with. Collect everyone's chart.

Activity

Museum Walk Display the completed Positive Assertiveness LSF Charts around the room or on tables. Students walk around and review all the charts. As they do, they draw a star next to any idea they connect with. Gather everyone together and invite volunteers to share their observations.

Reflection Gather everyone in a circle. Ask: "Think about your daily interactions with your peers here. Think about all the ideas shared today. What concrete actions can you do to ensure you're truly treating others with respect?"

*An LSF Chart template is available to download; see page 19.

Arrival Welcome

Greet each student by name as they enter.

Announcements

> Hello, Assertive Students!
>
> **Quote of the Day** "Strong people stand up for themselves. The strongest people stand up for others." —AUTHOR UNKNOWN
>
> Think about a time when you (or someone you knew) stood up for another person. Be ready to talk about that experience with your table group.

Point out today's (and/or this weekend's) key school and team events.

Acknowledgments

Around-the-Table Talk Hand out chart paper to each table group. Students greet their tablemates by name and then take turns sharing their experience in response to the announcements prompt. Then they discuss the responses to reach agreement on three to five positive strategies for standing up for someone else. A recorder from each group lists these on the chart paper.

TIP If students can't think of a time when they/someone they knew stood up for someone, or they prefer not to share that information publicly, suggest they consider a character from a book, movie, or TV show.

Activity

Creating a PSA (Public Service Announcement) Working with a partner or in small groups, students create a PSA (poster, radio, or TV ad) about standing up for others in positive ways. You may want to spread this activity out over several days of Advisory meetings so that students have time to plan, draft, revise, and rehearse it as needed. Encourage partnerships or groups to display or present their PSA to the whole group, then to the whole school, and finally to the wider community.

Reflection "Think about a rose, a thorn, and a bud. The rose is a positive experience you had this week, the thorn is a prickly experience you had this week, and the bud is something you're looking forward to this weekend." Invite a few students to share their rose, thorn, or bud.

Difficult Situations

Discuss and practice strategies for resolving challenging social situations

---

Skills Practiced This Week

Agree/disagree respectfully

Assertiveness

Compare/contrast

Cooperation

Problem-solving

DAY 1 ▪ Difficult Situations

Arrival Welcome

Greet each student by name as they enter. Remind students to read the announcements message.

Announcements

Welcome, Team!

This week you'll discuss how to handle difficult situations.

Fiona's Difficult Situation Fiona and her friend Mara have been practicing their soccer skills together all summer long. At tryouts, Mara says: "Let's promise we will only join the team if we both get accepted." Fiona says: "We've been working hard for this. If I get accepted, I'm joining no matter what." Mara says: "You're not a real friend if you join the team without me."

What advice would you give Fiona in this situation? What advice would you give Mara? Be ready to share.

Include upcoming school and team events in your messages this week.

Acknowledgments

Around-the-Table Chat Going clockwise around the table, students take turns sharing their advice for Fiona. Going counterclockwise, they take turns sharing their advice for Mara. Then they have a free-flowing conversation. Invite one member from each group to share a brief summary of their discussion with the whole group.

Activity

Ball Toss Use any kind of squishy ball or beach ball. Students stand at their desks or in a circle. Call out a topic: "Give an example of a difficult situation a student might face with a peer at school—for example, not agreeing on a topic for a class project." Then toss the ball to a student. The student who catches the ball shares an idea about that category, tosses the ball to someone else, and sits back down. After a few students give their ideas on a topic, change the category. The activity continues until everyone has had a turn or time is up.

Reflection "What is one thing you learned today that surprised you? What is one strategy you might try the next time you're in a similar situation?"

DAY 2 ■ Agree to Disagree

Arrival Welcome

Greet each student by name as they enter.

Announcements

> Hi, Classy Communicators!
>
> Have you heard the term "agree to disagree"? It's when two (or more) opposing sides come to an agreement that they disagree on a topic, and therefore, stop trying to convince the other side. For example: Devorah says a beach is the best vacation spot, but Zoe says a mountain is the best spot, so they agree to disagree.
>
> Think about this question: When might it be necessary to agree to disagree with someone?

Point out today's key school and team events.

Acknowledgments

Never-Ending Word Assign a recorder in each table group, and call out a category related to disagreement, such as "communication." Going around the table, each student thinks of a word that both fits into the category and starts with the last letter of the previous word said. The recorder writes down the words. After a few minutes, call on each table group to share their list. Display these lists and leave them up for the rest of this week's Advisory.

Never-Ending Word Example

Topic: Communicatio**n**

negotiat**e**

expres**s**

shar**e**

elaboratin**g**

genuine

Activity

Carousel Post chart paper around the room with the labels shown in the margin (one idea per chart), and give each group a different colored marker. In turn, groups visit one chart, brainstorm ideas for positive ways to address each side of the disagreement, and record their ideas on the chart. On your signal, groups rotate to the next chart and add to the listed ideas. Keep things moving by shortening rotation times as the process continues. Conclude once all groups have visited all charts.

Carousel Labels

➡ Disagree with project partner on research topic

➡ Disagree with parents about curfew/bedtime

➡ Disagree with friend about which movie to see

➡ Disagree with teacher about essay deadline

Reflection "Did you disagree with your groupmates during Never-Ending Word or Carousel? If so, how did you resolve your disagreements? How might the term 'agree to disagree' apply in one, some, or all of the Carousel chart topics?"

Difficult Situations

Discuss and practice strategies for resolving challenging social situations

---

DAY 3 ▪ Finding Middle Ground

Arrival Welcome

Greet each student by name as they enter. Encourage students to do a quick binder check as they get settled (see page 17).

Announcements

Hello, Agreeable Debaters!

"Finding middle ground" is when people who disagree find something to agree on.

Quote of the Day "It's a very important thing to learn to talk to those you disagree with." —PETE SEEGER, MUSICIAN

Think about the pros and cons of using personal technology in class. Be ready to share.

Point out today's key school and team events.

Acknowledgments

Debate Duos Students pair up and choose roles (or assign them yourself). Position A takes the "for" (or "pro") side and position B takes the "against" (or "con") side. Call out a topic: "Use of personal technology, such as smartphones or tablets, in the classroom." Give students some think time. Then signal to begin. Student A quickly names pros about the topic. After 30 seconds, signal student B to quickly name cons about the topic. Signal again to end this round. For the next round, pairs switch roles for the same topic. To wrap up, invite a few volunteers to share what it was like to debate both sides of the same topic.

Venn-ting Directions

After the pairs fill in their diagrams, the reporter from each pair roams the room looking at other diagrams while the presenter stays to explain their work to the other reporters. Allow reporters to visit two or three different diagrams and stay for 1–2 minutes at each. Reporters return to their original partners and discuss what they learned. Give students a few minutes to add to or revise their original diagrams.

Activity

Venn-ting State a "finding middle ground" scenario: "Imagine that Devorah and Zoe did not 'agree to disagree' on the best vacation spot. Help them find middle ground." Students pair up and choose roles (reporter, presenter). Each pair sets up and labels a Venn diagram "Beach," "Mountain," and "Both." State the number of similarities and differences that students should try to identify. (See next steps at left.)

Reflection "How did today's activities help find the middle ground of an argument? How might understanding an opposing side help in a disagreement?"

DAY 4 ▪ Success Through Cooperation

Arrival Welcome

Greet each student by name as they enter. Consider adding in a handshake.

Announcements

> Hello, Collaborative Class!
>
> You've learned some valuable tools to successfully navigate difficult situations and disagreements. Today you're going to put all your hard work to practice with some collaboration and cooperation.
>
> Think about what cooperation looks, sounds, and feels like.

Point out today's (and/or this weekend's) key school and team events.

Acknowledgments

Cooperative Sentences Each student writes down one word related to cooperation. Then as a table group, students work together to create a sentence or sentences (no more than a paragraph) using all their words. Each group shares their sentence(s), and the entire class takes some time to reflect in general about cooperation.

Activity

Three-Person Machine As a group, brainstorm different machines and tools used in daily life, and list them on chart paper. Students break into random groups of three and brainstorm how to pantomine a machine or tool from the list. Each group of three then demonstrates their machine for the rest of the students to guess.

Three-Person Machine Example

Car wash: Two students stand facing each other a few feet apart. They act as the washer by raising their hands overhead and wiggling their fingers to mimic water falling over the "car." The third student pantomimes driving the car while walking slowly between them.

Reflection Gather everyone in a circle. Ask: "Looking back on this week, how do communication and cooperation help people when they disagree? What is something you learned this week that might help you in the future?"

Walk the Talk

Clarify which qualities lead to success, and share through group presentation

Skills Practiced This Week

Cooperation
Making connections
Public speaking
Self-reflection

DAY 1 ■ Student Wanted, PART 1

Arrival Welcome

Greet each student by name as they enter. Remind students to read the announcements message.

Announcements

> Welcome, Clear Communicators!
>
> Do you know your ABCs?
>
> **Quote of the Day** "The ABCs are attitude, behavior, and communication skills." —GERALD CHERTAVIAN, FOUNDER OF YEAR UP
>
> Take an I Am/We Are ABCs list. Write down the qualities that make up your own Attitude, Behavior, and Communication skills (such as having a positive attitude, being kind to others, and being an active listener). Be ready to share.

Include upcoming school and team events in your messages this week.

Acknowledgments

I Am/We Are Students pair up and compare their I Am/We Are ABCs* lists. Let students know that they can add new ideas to their list. Each pair joins another pair to identify commonalities on their lists and create a We Are ABCs list. Students display their We Are ABCs, where everyone can see them. Each group of four stays together.

Activity

Student Wanted Ad, Part 1 Each group reviews the other groups' lists. They star any idea all group members connect to. Then everyone creates a whole-group We Are ABCs list. Each group goes back to their table to brainstorm and choose their group's number-one ABC skill from the whole-group list. Collect each group's ABC.

Reflection "The group you're in will be your communications group for the rest of the week. Think about your group's number-one ABC and why these traits are important. Tomorrow you're going to create a Student Wanted Ad using these traits."

*An I Am/We Are ABCs list is available to download; see page 19.

DAY 2 ■ Student Wanted, PART 2

Arrival Welcome

Greet each student by name as they enter. Consider adding in a high five.

Announcements

> Hi, Team!
>
> Yesterday you came up with the ABCs of our Advisory group. Today you're going to use these ABCs to create a Student Wanted Ad—specifically an ad for the type of communication skills needed to succeed in our Advisory.
>
> Review your group's number-one ABC from yesterday. Think about (1) why these specific traits are important, and (2) catchy phrases from ads you've seen, heard, or read. Be ready to share with your group.

Point out today's key school and team events.

Acknowledgments

Group Brainstorm Students get into their communications group from yesterday and greet each other by name. Going clockwise, they share their response to #1 of the announcements prompt. Going counterclockwise, they share their response to #2. Then they brainstorm how to incorporate these ideas into their Student Wanted Ad. Students stay in their communications group.

Activity

Student Wanted Ad, Part 2 Hand each group chart paper or poster board and markers to create a Student Wanted Ad that describes the qualities that an ideal student should have in Advisory. Emphasize that students should reference their group's number-one ABC. Then collect everyone's Student Wanted Ads and tell students they'll create a one-minute speech to promote their ads in tomorrow's Advisory.

Reflection "In what ways did your group demonstrate your number-one ABC in today's Advisory?"

Walk the Talk

Clarify which qualities lead to success, and share through group presentation

DAY 3 ■ 100 Words Plus

Arrival Welcome

Greet each student by name as they enter. Encourage students to do a quick binder check as they get settled (see page 17).

Announcements

Hello, Speech Writers!

On average, a person can speak 125–150 words a minute. Today you're going to write a 1-minute speech to go with your Student Wanted Ads.

Quote of the Day "It usually takes me three weeks to write a good impromptu speech." —MARK TWAIN, AUTHOR, HUMORIST

Get your communications group's number-one ABC from yesterday. Think about the promotional tactics, such as pace, tone, and message, of an ad. When might someone choose to use more words in a 1-minute speech? Fewer words? Be ready to share with your group.

Point out today's key school and team events.

Acknowledgments

Around-the-Table Chat Assign each group a facilitator. One by one, students greet their tablemates and briefly discuss their response to the announcements prompt about using more words. Going in turn, students briefly explain their response to using fewer words. Then students brainstorm how many words they want to use for their one-minute speech, based on the message they want to convey for their Student Wanted Ad.

Activity

NOTE Brainwriting is writing down ideas before sharing them aloud.

Speech Brainwrite On their own, students write down their ideas to include in their group's one-minute speech. Going in turn, they share one idea until all ideas are heard. As a group, they choose at least two ideas from each group member. Each group member writes a sentence or two about their ideas. From these sentences, the group writes their one-minute speech (using at least 100 words but no more than 150).

Reflection "How did you communicate your ideas in your group today? How did you come to an agreement about which ideas to include in your speech?"

Arrival Welcome

Greet each student by name as they enter.

Announcements

> Congrats, Advisory Team!
>
> You've worked so hard at communicating about communicating this week. Today you're going to show off your speaking and listening skills.
>
> Meet with your group and time your speech. Is it under 1 minute? Be ready to share your speech today with the whole group!

Point out today's (and/or this weekend's) key school and team events.

One-Minute Speech Presentation Options

Instead of live presentations, students could create:

➡ Podcasts

➡ Videos

➡ Audio recordings

➡ Online presentations

Acknowledgments

One-Minute Speech In turn, each group holds up their Student Wanted Ad and presents their one-minute speech to the whole group. After all groups present, display everyone's ads. Gather students and have them share their observations about the ABCs they chose and how they can each demonstrate these "Student Wanted" traits in Advisory.

Activity

Walk, Stop Round 1: When you call out "Walk," students walk around the room. When you call out "Stop," they stop where they are and greet someone next to them by name. Call out "Walk" and "Stop" several times, varying the speed of when you call out the commands. Round 2: Switch the commands so that when you say "Stop," students walk, and when you say "Walk," students stop. Repeat commands several times (similar to Round 1). Round 3: Add two more commands: "Clap" (students clap once) and "Name" (students say their name). Note: "Walk" and "Stop" commands are still reversed. Round 4: Switch up the second set of commands so that "Clap" means "Name" and "Name" means "Clap" (now all four spoken commands require their opposite action).

Reflection Gather everyone in a circle. Ask: "How does Walk, Stop work as an example of communication? Why do you think ABCs are important in our interactions with each other? Moving forward, how can we work on maintaining our own ABCs inside and outside of school?"

Interviewing School Leaders

Interview members of school staff to learn qualities of an effective leader

---

Skills Practiced This Week

Active listening

Asking/answering questions thoughtfully

Leadership

Making connections

Organization

TIPS Interview Planning

➡ Inform other teachers, administrators, and school staff ahead of time that students might be requesting short interviews with them this week.

➡ Once you know who students will be interviewing, give these school leaders a heads-up so that they can plan for the interview.

DAY 1 ■ School Leaders You Admire

Arrival Welcome

Greet each student by name as they enter. Remind students to read the announcements message.

Announcements

Hello, Team!

To admire someone means to have respect for them, to look up to them. This week, you'll be planning interviews with school leaders you admire. These leaders may be teachers, counselors, administrators, or other school staff. They may be leaders you have worked with or leaders you will work with next year.

Think of a school leader you want to interview. What do you admire about them? Be ready to share.

Include upcoming school and team events in your messages this week.

Acknowledgments

Around-the-Table Sharing Students greet each of their tablemates by name. Then they take turns sharing their response to the announcements prompt. Write these down. Tell students you will inform the school leaders they chose that students will be interviewing them in the near future.

Activity

Word Splash In their table group, students create a Word Splash* about the qualities of the school leaders they admire. Then each group presents and explains their Word Splash. Display the Word Splashes where everyone can see them.

Reflection "What are some similarities among the qualities of all the school leaders you admire? How do these school leaders positively influence your life?"

*A Word Splash template and example are available to download; see page 19.

DAY 2 ▪ Planning the Interview

Arrival Welcome

Greet each student by name as they enter.

Announcements

Hi, Planners!

Today you're going to plan your school leader interviews.

What do you already know about the school leader you chose yesterday? Be ready to share with a partner.

Point out today's key school and team events.

Acknowledgments

Interview At tables, students pair up, greet their partner by name, and take turns interviewing each other about their response to the announcements prompt. Students then take turns interviewing the other members of their table group about their response. Ask a few volunteers to share their group's ideas with the whole group.

Activity

Swap Meet On their own, students write down questions about what they would like to learn about their school leader. For example, for a music teacher, a student might write "What inspired you to teach music?" Then they share their questions with their tablemates. Encourage students to write down any of their tablemates' ideas that they connect with. Ask each group to share one or two questions with the whole group. Have students put their names on their lists and collect them. Students will use these in tomorrow's Advisory.

Reflection "How did reflecting on what you already know about your school leader help you formulate questions for your interview? How did hearing your peers' ideas influence your interview questions?"

Interviewing School Leaders

Interview members of school staff to learn qualities of an effective leader

---

DAY 3 ■ How Would You Interview?

Arrival Welcome

Greet each student by name as they enter. Encourage students to do a quick binder check as they get settled (see page 17).

Announcements

> Hello, Interviewers!
>
> There are different ways to conduct an interview. It can be done in person, by telephone, through email, or by video chat.
>
> Get your list of questions from yesterday. Think about the best way to interview your school leader. Be ready to share your ideas.

Point out today's key school and team events.

Acknowledgments

Partner Chat With their interview partner from yesterday, students share their ideas in response to the announcements prompt. Then they examine their interview questions and help each other narrow down their list to three to five questions. Partners stay together.

Carousel Examples

➡ **In person:** Jot down notes to remember key information

➡ **Telephone:** Ask clarifying questions when you need more information

➡ **Email:** List questions in bullet form

➡ **Video chat:** Use a neutral background such as a blank wall to avoid distractions

Activity

Carousel Post chart paper (one idea per chart) in each corner of the room with the labels shown at left, providing an example for each one. Partners rotate to each chart, brainstorm ideas for how they would conduct their interview using that chart's method, and list their ideas on the chart. Signal when it's time for partners to rotate to keep things moving so each pair can contribute ideas to each chart. Discuss the charts as a whole group as time allows. Keep charts displayed. Students will use them tomorrow.

Reflection Have students review each chart on their own and star ideas they connect to. Ask: "How can these ideas help you choose which method to use for your interview?"

DAY 4 ■ Future Leaders

Arrival Welcome

Greet each student by name as they enter. Consider also giving a handshake.

Announcements

> Congrats, Future Leaders!
>
> Are you ready to conduct your interviews? What interview method will you use?
>
> **Quote of the Day** "Leadership and learning are indispensable to each other." —JOHN F. KENNEDY, 35TH PRESIDENT OF THE UNITED STATES
>
> What does this quote mean to you? Be ready to share.

Point out today's (and/or this weekend's) key school and team events.

Acknowledgments

Hand Up, Pair Up Rounds 1–2: Students find a partner from a different table group, give a high five, and share their response to the announcements prompt. Round 3: Students find a partner from a different table group, give a high five, and share which school leader they're going to interview and the interview method they chose (in person, by email, etc.).

Activity

NOTE Have students set up and conduct their interviews. Students will share what they learned from these interviews on Day 1 of the "Student-Led Advisory Planning" Advisory week on page 92).

Four Corners Designate one corner of the room for each method (in person, by telephone, through email, by video chat). Students move to the corner of the room that represents their method of interview and share their answers to the following questions: (1) How will you introduce yourself to the interviewee? (2) What type of communication skills should you keep in mind when conducting the interview? (3) How will you record the interviewee's answers during the interview? Emphasize that students can reference the Carousel charts from yesterday.

Reflection Gather students together in a circle. Ask: "What is one key idea you learned this week while planning your interviews? How do you think planning and conducting an interview will help you strengthen your leadership skills?"

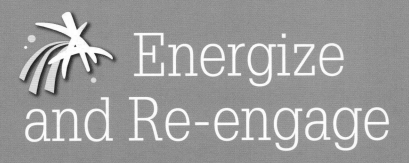

Energize and Re-engage

4-Day Plans

Tips for Energizing and Re-engaging Students

All Grades

To keep students energized, it's essential to address their basic physical needs for activity, food, and rest. Be mindful of their energy levels during Advisory. Early mornings might call for recharging activities to help students get ready for the day. Or, if you meet after a high-energy period like lunch, refocusing activities might help them get back into academics.

Self-control can be especially hard during physical and developmental growth spurts. Encourage students to practice calming strategies, such as slow, deep breathing.

Being a calm and supportive presence while giving students outlets to voice their opinions, shape classroom routines (where appropriate), and debate respectfully will help keep them engaged in classroom life.

Grade Six

Though moving steadily toward greater independence, sixth graders may still need adult support with time management and homework skills. Work with students to identify times when they are able to stay organized and motivated (and strategies for doing so), and times when a teacher or parent could support them.

Sixth graders enjoy games, puzzles, and brain teasers, and they like to measure their personal best. They also enjoy playing as a team and may be energized by collaborative games that challenge them and help them connect with their peers.

In addition, students have an appreciation for humor, so incorporating some lightheartedness into Advisory and allowing students to express their own sense of humor can keep the energy level in the room high.

Grade Seven

Enthusiastic and spontaneous, seventh graders are trying on different personas as they find their way toward their own adult personality. They love playing and inventing games, word play, new vocabulary, and conversation with both adults and peers. Help them get energized through playful opportunities to explore new interests.

Students in this age group are great classroom collaborators and study group partners, especially when they can choose their own partners and topics of conversation. Invite them to brainstorm ways they can motivate themselves and each other. Capture these ideas and display them for reference.

Seventh graders are getting better at handling multiple-day assignments. However, following through on practice and completing projects that span weekends may still be challenging. Help them get and stay focused through the use of weekly or monthly planners.

Grade Eight

Eighth graders may question their teachers and the purpose of what they're learning. Offering calm and thoughtful answers and connecting classroom content to the larger world can help students stay engaged with academics.

Students at this age are more sensitive to criticism and more hesitant to take academic risks. However, they are interested in thinking about issues from many sides, particularly topics related to fairness and justice. Pairing them with a single partner to discuss these topics can invigorate them.

Eighth graders may be more vulnerable to peer pressure and have stronger opinions about school subjects they do or don't like. Keep them invested and focused by having them help build rubrics for evaluating their own work.

Life Stories, Take 2

Strengthen the Advisory community by learning about multiple perspectives and sharing interests

Skills Practiced This Week

Drawing conclusions

Organization

Teamwork

Understanding multiple perspectives

Fact or Fiction Example

➔ Josh from *The Crossover* by Kwame Alexander has a twin brother named Alex [F].

➔ Josh plays basketball [T].

➔ Josh has to cut his hair after losing a bet [T].

NOTE Students will reference their Life Story* from the "Life Story" Advisory week on pages 33–39.

Collect everyone's Life Story to use on Day 3.

DAY 1 ▪ What a Character!

Arrival Welcome

Greet each student by name as they enter. Remind students to read the announcements message.

Announcements

> Welcome, Fiction (and Nonfiction) Fans!
>
> This week you're going to take a step back and think about the Life Stories you created.
>
> Get your Life Story. Think about your favorite book character from section #1 (or choose a different character). List five qualities about this character that you admire. Be ready to share.

Include upcoming school and team events in your messages this week.

Acknowledgments

One-Minute Greeting Students greet as many people as they can in one minute. Consider joining in the greeting. Then in their table group, students share their response to the announcements prompt and identify any commonalities.

Activity

Fact or Fiction On an index card, students list their favorite character, the book title, and three statements about their character: two are factual (true) and one is fictional (false). (Consider completing a card with your favorite character from your Life Story.*) Then one student reads their statements (see example in margin). The other students vote on which statement they think is false. The student who read reveals the false one and turns it into a true statement: "Josh has a twin brother named JB." Continue until everyone has shared, or spread this activity over several Advisory meetings.

Reflection "What have you learned about your classmates and yourself based on their book character choices?"

*A Life Story template is available to download; see page 19.

Book Meets Book

Arrival Welcome

Greet each student by name as they enter. Consider adding in a handshake or a high five.

Announcements

> Hi, Avid Readers!
>
> **Quote of the Day** "I know that books seem like the ultimate thing that's made by one person, but that's not true. Every reading of a book is a collaboration between the reader and the writer who are making the story up together." —JOHN GREEN, AUTHOR
>
> Think about what this quote means to you. Be ready to share.

Point out today's key school and team events.

Acknowledgments

Around-the-Table Sharing Going around the table, students greet each other by name and share their response to the announcements prompt. Then students pair up to share their favorite character from yesterday. Each student takes a few minutes on their own to write three to five questions that their character might ask their partner's character in an interview. For example: Dorothy from *The Wonderful Wizard of Oz* might ask Alice from *Alice's Adventures in Wonderland* if Alice still visits her friends in Wonderland.

Activity

Interview Using the questions they generated during acknowledgments, students take turns interviewing their partner's character from their character's point of view (see example in margin). Then pairs share one idea their partner shared with the whole group.

Interview Example

- Student 1 might ask: "Alice wants to know: How would Dorothy handle the Queen of Hearts' quick temper?"

- Student 2 responds: "First, Dorothy would tell the Queen of Hearts that she was scaring other people. Then she would ask why she was so angry, and help her find a way to calm herself down."

Reflection "How did you use what you knew about your favorite character to answer your partner's questions? What did you learn about your favorite character that you hadn't thought about before?"

Life Stories, Take 2

Strengthen the Advisory community by learning about multiple perspectives and sharing interests

---

Humdingers Song Ideas

➔ Itsy, Bitsy Spider

➔ Old MacDonald

➔ Row, Row, Row Your Boat

➔ The Wheels on the Bus

➔ Twinkle, Twinkle, Little Star

DAY 3 ▪ Band Together, PART 1

Arrival Welcome

Greet each student by name as they enter.

Announcements

Hello, Music Enthusiasts!

Quote of the Day "Music is the greatest communication in the world."
—LOU RAWLS, MUSICIAN

Get your Life Story from yesterday. Then think about this question: How does music connect you to other people? Be ready to share.

Point out today's key school and team events.

Acknowledgments

Humdingers Hand students strips of paper, each with the title of one of four well-known pop songs (or childhood songs; see ideas at left). Students hum their song while they safely move about the room listening for others who are humming the same song. (Consider joining in.) When they find a match, they stand together and hum the song in unison until four groups have formed, each humming a different song. Then students share their response to the announcements prompt with their groupmates.

Activity

A Day in Harmony, Part 1 Give each group chart paper, and designate one person as the recorder. Group members share the musical group they'd like to spend the day with (from their Life Story* section #2) and agree on one musical group to visit the school. Individually, students list ideas for how to plan the school visit, circle their top three ideas, and take turns nominating each one for consensus. If all members agree on the idea, the recorder lists it on the chart paper. The activity ends when the group has listed three to five consensus ideas. Collect each group's chart for use tomorrow.

Reflection "What do you think Lou Rawls meant when he said, 'Music is the greatest communication in the world'?"

*A Life Story template is available to download; see page 19.

Band Together, PART 2

Arrival Welcome

Greet each student by name as they enter. Encourage students to do a quick binder check as they get settled (see page 17).

Announcements

> Rock On, Event Planners!
>
> Today you're going to use your ideas from yesterday to plan a school visit from the musical group your group chose.
>
> Get your chart paper from yesterday. Think about how you'd plan one of your top ideas. Be ready to share with your group from yesterday.

Point out today's (and/or this weekend's) key school and team events.

Acknowledgments

Group Brainstorm Group members greet each other by name and then review the top three to five ideas on their chart paper, brainstorming ways they could use these ideas to plan their musical group's school visit. Then they take a vote to decide on the top two ideas.

Activity

A Day in Harmony, Part 2 Students create a poster, bulletin board, or slide show advertising "A Day in Harmony" with their musical group. It should include the musical group's name, the date of the event, the day's agenda, and any other information they feel is relevant. Students present their finished product to the whole group and take comments and questions.

Reflection Gather everyone in a circle. Ask: "What did you learn about teamwork while planning your event with your group? What did you learn about yourself?"

Strengthening Self-Control

Devise strategies for, and experience the impact of, slowing down and thinking before speaking or acting

---

Skills Practiced This Week

Asking for help
Responsibility
Self-awareness
Self-control
Speaking essentials

DAY 1 ■ # What Is Self-Control?

Arrival Welcome

Greet each student by name as they enter. Remind students to read the announcements message.

Announcements

Welcome, Students!

One definition of self-control is the ability to recognize and regulate one's own thoughts, emotions, and behaviors in any situation.

What does the term "self-control" mean to you? Be ready to share your thoughts with your table group.

Include upcoming school and team events in your messages this week.

Acknowledgments

Around-the-Table Chat Going clockwise around the table, students greet their tablemates by name and share their response to the announcements prompt. Going counterclockwise, students share one example of demonstrating self-control, such as walking down the hall when you want to run.

Activity

Shake It Down Everyone stands while the leader counts out loud from 1 to 16. On each count up to 16, everyone raises their right hand and shakes it. Then to the same count, they shake their left hand, then their right foot, and finally their left foot. Next the leader calls out "Cut" or "Slice" and cuts the count in half. On each count from 1 to 8, everyone shakes their right hand, their left hand, their right foot, and their left foot. The leader cuts the count to 4, then 2, and finally 1. To end the activity, the leader calls out "Shake it down!" and everyone shakes their whole body.

Reflection Gather everyone in a circle. Ask: "How does self-control play a role during an activity like Shake It Down? Why is it important to have self-control?"

DAY 2 ▪ It's Time to Begin

Arrival Welcome

Greet each student by name as they enter.

Announcements

> Hi, Thoughtful Communicators!
>
> Today you're going to explore how self-control plays a part in being a thoughtful communicator. Do you know the saying "Think before you speak"?
>
> On a sticky note, write down the very first thing that comes to mind right now. Do not put your name on it, and keep it to yourself.

Point out today's key school and team events.

Acknowledgments

Silent Quotes Hand each student a half quote from the Silent Quotes* handout (or make your own). Students silently move around the room searching for their match. With their matching partner, they read the whole quote and discuss its meaning. Have a few pairs share their quote with the whole group.

Activity

Graffiti Post chart paper around the room with the headings shown at left (or similar ones). Students "graffiti" their ideas on the charts (starting at any chart, going in any order, writing in any style anywhere on the chart). Then assign small groups to find common themes and trends among the ideas on each chart. Each group shares a summary of their findings with the whole group. Post the completed charts for reference this week.

Reflection Invite students to post their sticky note responses to the announcements prompt by the Graffiti charts. Ask: "How does thinking before you speak make you a thoughtful communicator?"

*A Silent Quotes template and example are available to download; see page 19.

Graffiti Headings

➥ "Think before you speak" means . . .

➥ What's one way self-control is important for communication?

➥ What are some situations in which it's especially important to think before you speak?

➥ What can you do if you say something that you didn't mean to say?

Strengthening Self-Control

Devise strategies for, and experience the impact of, slowing down and thinking before speaking or acting

DAY 3 ■ Check Yourself

Arrival Welcome

Greet each student by name as they enter. Encourage students to do a quick binder check as they get settled (see page 17).

Announcements

> Hello, Team!
>
> Today you're going to practice putting self-control into action.
>
> What are some common struggles with maintaining self-control (for example, blurting out answers)? Write down 1 or 2 ideas to share, on separate index cards, and hand your card(s) to me.

Point out today's key school and team events.

Acknowledgments

Standing Partner Chat Students pair up and spread out around the room. They greet each other by name, take turns sharing their responses to the announcements prompt, and discuss why they think these are common struggles.

Activity

World Café* Assign each table a facilitator and give them an index card from the announcements prompt (for example, slamming doors when angry). Students discuss different strategies that might help someone overcome that struggle (for example, counting to 10). After 2–3 minutes, signal to wrap up conversations. Everyone except the facilitator changes tables. The facilitator shares the previous group's struggle and summarizes the strategies discussed. Then the new group discusses their own ideas. When you signal again, each group chooses a new facilitator for their table before moving on to the next one. Repeat with new index cards as time allows.

Reflection Gather everyone in a circle. Ask: "How might knowing all these different strategies help people better gain self-control?"

*This is an adaptation of the World Café™, a structured conversational process found at www.theworldcafe.com.

> **TIP**
>
> **Meeting One-on-One With Your Advisees**
>
> You can use this time to pair up with one advisee to get to know them better and continue to strengthen your relationship with them.

DAY 4 ■ Maintaining Self-Control

Arrival Welcome

Greet each student by name as they enter.

Announcements

> Congrats, Advisory Team!
>
> You've worked hard to strengthen your self-control!
>
> Keep this to yourself: Think of your personal struggles with maintaining self-control. Then think of 2 people you trust (1 person outside of school and 1 person at school) who could help you stay on track with your self-control.

Point out today's (and/or this weekend's) key school and team events.

Acknowledgments

Word Splash In their table group, students greet each other by name and create a Word Splash* about self-control. Then each group presents and explains their Word Splash. Display students' Word Splashes where everyone can see them.

Activity

Transformation In this version of Rock-Paper-Scissors, four beings transform as follows: Egg to Chicken to Dragon to Invincible. Only similar beings can play each other—until they become Invincible and can play anyone. Everyone starts as an Egg, finds a partner, and plays Rock-Paper-Scissors. The student who wins becomes a Chicken; the other student stays an Egg. Each being transforms up or down, accordingly, for each round. While finding partners, students move according to their being (see descriptions at left). Once students become Invincible, they stay Invincible and can play against any being (if the other being wins the round, they also become Invincible).

Transformation Moves

- **Egg** squats down
- **Chicken** hunches with arms crooked like chicken wings
- **Dragon** stands with arms outstretched, as if flying
- **Invincible** stands tall with hands on hips, elbows pointing out from sides

Reflection "Think of the strategies you've discussed this week to help you better gain self-control. How will you keep yourself accountable? How might you ask the people you trust to help you stay on track?"

*A Word Splash template and example are available to download; see page 19.

Motivation 2.0

Brainstorm how to stay motivated and identify people who can help with this goal

Skills Practiced This Week

Goal-setting
Helping others
Problem-solving
Self-motivation
Self-reflection

DAY 1 ▪ Zap Motivation Zappers

Arrival Welcome

Greet each student by name as they enter. Remind students to read the announcements message.

Announcements

Welcome, Team!

Can you believe this is the last week of the quarter? This week will focus on how to stay motivated so you can finish strong!

What zaps your motivation? Take an index card and write down 1 or 2 motivation zappers. Be ready to share.

Include upcoming school and team events in your messages this week.

Acknowledgments

Mix and Mingle to Music Play upbeat music as students walk around the room, holding their index cards from the announcements prompt. When you stop the music, students greet each other by name, offer a handshake or another friendly gesture, and exchange a motivation zapper. After about 30 seconds, start the music again. Repeat so that students greet at least four classmates; then they return to their table group. Collect everyone's index cards.

Activity

Six Corners (a version of Four Corners) Display six motivation zappers from students' cards around the room and read them out loud. Give students a moment to choose one zapper and move to that corner. Students form pairs or small groups to discuss different strategies that might help someone overcome the motivation zapper they chose. After 2–3 minutes, signal to wrap up conversations. Everyone chooses a new zapper, moves to its corresponding area, and discusses it. Repeat as time allows.

Reflection "What have you learned about your classmates today? Yourself? How can this knowledge help you stay motivated?"

DAY 2 ■ Motivation Strategies

Arrival Welcome

Greet each student by name as they enter.

Announcements

Hello, Advisors!

Roland's Story, Part 1 Roland wants to be a microbiologist, and he's worked hard to keep his grades up. But now that spring has arrived, Roland's motivation to study is zapped. All he wants to do is be outside with his friends.

What advice would you give Roland to help him stay motivated? Be ready to share.

Point out today's key school and team events.

Acknowledgments

One-Minute Greeting Students greet as many people as they can in one minute. When time is up, they partner with the last person they greeted and share their response to the announcements prompt. Tell students they'll read Part 2 of Roland's Story on Day 4 and to stay with their partner for the Graffiti activity.

Graffiti Headings

→ What advice would you give Roland?

→ How might Roland's friends help him stay motivated?

→ What is your biggest motivation zapper?

→ What motivates you?

Activity

Tag Team Graffiti Post chart paper around the room with the headings shown at left. Tag Teams (pairs from acknowledgments) brainstorm ideas and "graffiti" them on the charts (starting at any chart, going in any order, writing in any style anywhere on the chart). Then they partner with another Tag Team to find connections among the ideas. Each group summarizes their findings for the whole group. Keep the charts displayed all week.

Reflection "Rate your motivation as an individual team member in today's Advisory from 1 (low) to 5 (high). How important is each individual team member's level of motivation to a team's success, and why?"

Motivation 2.0

Brainstorm how to stay motivated and identify people who can help with this goal

DAY 3 ■ Motivation Coach

Arrival Welcome

Greet each student by name as they enter. Encourage students to do a quick binder check as they get settled (see page 17).

Announcements

Hello, Motivators!

Sometimes, just knowing what zaps your motivation—and learning strategies to overcome it—is enough to stay motivated! Other times, we need a little more support.

Quote of the Day "If you want to go quickly, go alone. If you want to go far, go together." —PROVERB

Think about a time when someone gave you a pep talk that helped motivate you. Be ready to share.

Point out today's key school and team events.

Acknowledgments

Around-the-Table Chat In their table group, students greet each other by name and go around the table sharing their response to the announcements prompt. Then they have a free-flowing discussion about why they felt motivated by that experience. Ask a few volunteers to share their experiences with the whole group.

Activity

Creating a SMART Goal Plan Students pair up with their Tag Team partner from yesterday. Hand each pair a SMART goal sheet* and explain that they'll be each other's motivation coach for the next few weeks. Guide students in how to use their SMART goal sheets to create a plan to help each other stay motivated. Then pairs share one way they're going to motivate each other with the whole group.

Reflection Gather everyone in a circle. Ask: "What does today's quote mean to you? How does it apply to teaming up with someone and being their motivation coach?"

*A SMART goal template is available to download; see page 19.

Power Up

Arrival Welcome

Greet each student by name as they enter. Consider also giving a sincere compliment ("Camila, I admire how you stand up for others").

Announcements

Congrats, Energized Team!

Roland's Story, Part 2 To stay motivated, Roland started a study group with his friends at his local park. For every 20 minutes of homework time, they "power up" with a few free throws on the basketball court. When they finish up their work, they play a pickup basketball game.

When you need a quick motivator, what do you do to power up? Be ready to share.

Point out today's (and/or this weekend's) key school and team events.

Acknowledgments

Partner Chat Students greet their motivation coach partner (from Day 3) by name and share their response to the announcements prompt.

Activity

Ma Zinga Students stand next to their partner in a circle and take turns sharing their partner's response to the announcements prompt. Then everyone points their arms into the middle of the circle. Choose a student to be the leader. The group says "Maaa . . ." with the "ah" sound gradually rising as students shake their fingers, hands, and arms to build up energy. At the leader's signal—a nod of the head—the group quickly pulls back their hands while forming fists and cheers "Zinga!" loudly together. Repeat with a new leader as time allows.

Reflection Post an anchor chart labeled "Stick With It." Ask: "Looking back on this week, what's your number-one motivational strategy you'll stick with for the rest of the year? Write your response on a sticky note and post it on our Stick With It chart." Have students view everyone's responses and share their observations. Keep the chart displayed for students to reference.

Finishing the Year Strong

Reflect on academic achievements and personal growth to pinpoint strategies that lead to success

---

Skills Practiced This Week

Exchanging ideas

Evaluating

Perseverance

Self-reflection

Maître d' Examples

➡ **Table for 3:** What does academic achievement look, sound, and feel like?

➡ **Table for 4:** What's one strategy that helps you achieve your goals?

➡ **Table for 2:** What is one academic goal you would like to set for next year?

DAY 1 ■ Academic Highlights of the Year

Arrival Welcome

Greet each student by name as they enter. Remind students to read the announcements message.

Announcements

> Salutations, Savvy Students!
>
> You've accomplished so much to be proud of this year.
>
> Think about all the work you've done. What's one academic achievement that really sticks out to you? Why?

Include upcoming school and team events in your messages this week.

Acknowledgments

One-Sentence Sharing In their table group, students greet each other and take turns sharing a one-sentence response to the announcements prompt. For example: "One academic achievement I'm proud of is my school leader interview with Mr. Moran. I learned why he became a science teacher, and I discovered that I really like to conduct interviews." Listen in and note some achievements.

Activity

Maître d' Call out a table grouping (for example: "Table for 3!"). Students quickly form standing groups of that number to discuss their responses to a question you pose (see examples in margin). Give students 1–2 minutes to share. Repeat as time allows, continuing to vary the table size.

Reflection "What did you learn about yourself during today's activities? How does reflecting on your achievements help in planning future goals?"

Personal Highlights of the Year

Arrival Welcome

Greet each student by name as they enter. Consider adding in a handshake or a high five.

Announcements

> Hi, Team!
>
> Yesterday you talked about your academic achievements. Today you're going to highlight personal achievements of the year.
>
> What's one personal goal you achieved this year? Be ready to share.

Point out today's key school and team events.

Acknowledgments

What's the News? In their table group, one student begins by greeting the student to their left by saying "Good morning, _____. What's the news?" The student greeted responds with "Good morning _____. The news is [student shares their response from the announcements prompt]." Continue around the table until all students have shared their response.

Activity

Fact or Fiction Students write three statements about their personal achievements over the year: two are factual (true); one is fictional (false). For example: "I read eight novels this year [T]. I learned to ride a unicycle [F]. I learned CPR [T]." Choose the first student to read their statements. The other students vote on which statement they think is false, and then the reader reveals the false one. Continue until everyone has shared, or spread this activity over several Advisory meetings.

Reflection Have students pair up with someone who achieved a similar personal goal and briefly discuss why they set out to accomplish it.

Finishing the Year Strong

Reflect on academic achievements and personal growth to pinpoint strategies that lead to success

DAY 3 ■ Self-Reflection

Arrival Welcome

Greet each student by name as they enter. Encourage students to do a quick binder check as they get settled (see page 17).

Announcements

Hello, Independent Thinkers!

Quote of the Day "To be yourself in a world that is constantly trying to make you something else is the greatest accomplishment."
—RALPH WALDO EMERSON, WRITER, PHILOSOPHER

What have you learned about yourself this year? How have you changed? Take some time to think about this.

Point out today's key school and team events.

Acknowledgments

Snowball Students write down their anonymous response to the announcements prompt on a piece of paper and crumple it into a "snowball." Then they form a circle and gently toss their snowball into the center. Students pick up one snowball near them and read aloud what's on the paper. Collect all the snowballs.

Activity

Just Like Me Use what students wrote on the snowballs to create prompts. As you say each prompt, students who feel it applies to them stand up (or raise hands if standing is difficult) and say "Just like me" at the same time. Take time to observe who does and who does not stand up (or who doesn't stand up as often), and check in with them to hear their ideas. Repeat for as many rounds as time allows.

Reflection Gather everyone in a circle. Ask: "What does the Quote of the Day mean to you?"

Just Like Me Prompt Ideas

- I'm more confident as a writer [student, artist, friend] now.
- Now I know how to set goals and how to reach them.
- I improved my skills in math [science, social studies, English].

DAY 4 ■ Strategies to Finish the Year Strong

Arrival Welcome

Greet each student by name as they enter.

Announcements

> Greetings, Fine Finishers!
>
> There are only 2 more weeks of school! Can you believe it? Today you're going to make a plan to finish the year strong.
>
> **Quote of the Day** "There are better starters than me, but I'm a strong finisher." —USAIN BOLT, OLYMPIC GOLD MEDALIST
>
> Think of some strategies or tips you've learned this year (motivational tips, study strategies, communication skills) that have helped you succeed in a particular area. Be ready to share a few.

Point out today's (and/or this weekend's) key school and team events.

Acknowledgments

Inside-Outside Circles Students count off by twos. Ones form an inner circle and face out; twos form an outer circle and face in to form pairs. Partners greet each other by name and share one or two sentences about a strategy or tip that has helped them succeed. Then twos move one person to their right, greet their new partner, and share the same strategy or tip, or a new one. Continue until everyone has shared with three to five partners.

Activity

Quote Makers Using the strategies and tips they heard during acknowledgments as inspiration, students work in small groups to create at least one quote to inspire other students to finish the year strong. To give their quote more impact, they also create a brief skit or song to go along with it. Then each group presents their skit or song to the whole group. Display the quotes on an anchor chart for inspiration for the rest of the year.

Reflection Gather everyone in a circle. Ask: "How can you stay strong as a team over the next two weeks? How can you stay inspired to finish the year strong?"

Reflect and Recalibrate

4-Day Plans

Tips for Reflecting and Recalibrating

All Grades

During exams or at the end of the quarter, students may be feeling more stress and anxiety about tests, papers, projects, and grades. But they may be just as stressed and anxious about social pressures and the ebb and flow of friendships and other relationships. Giving some "quiet time" to pause and refresh can provide a welcome break from stressful academics and social dynamics.

As a new quarter begins, encourage students to reflect on their successes and struggles from the previous quarter. Guide them to regroup after setbacks, figure out what really motivates them, learn to persevere, and build their growth mindset.

Toward the end of the year, provide opportunities to come together and recognize all the collaborative work students have done in Advisory and celebrate it!

Grade Six

Sixth graders are starting to be able to see things from new perspectives, and they can benefit from brief discussions about consequences. Hearing a variety of perspectives from classmates helps them reflect on different points of view and consider how their actions can affect others.

Students are generally more interested in learning new things than in reviewing or revising older work. Guide them not just to revise their work but to reflect upon the value of revision in general. Take advantage of their desire to measure their individual best performance to frame discussions about improving upon their work.

Whole-group meetings and peer mediation can be effective techniques for resolving issues among sixth graders. Use these practices as opportunities to reflect on what is working well in the group or in specific situations, and to see where there could be room for improvement.

Grade Seven

Seventh graders make great peer reviewers and project partners. Partner or small-group discussions offer students the opportunity to reflect on their work together and strengthen their skills.

Students this age are trying out new interests as their adult personalities begin to emerge, so encourage them to try new clubs, groups, and extracurricular activities. Help them reflect on what they like, where their natural skills are, and how they might apply those skills and interests in the future. Joining new activities will also give students the chance to connect with various adults in the school who can help them reflect on challenging situations and make good choices.

Seventh graders appreciate teachers who listen and take their suggestions seriously, so work with students to recalibrate routines in ways that make sense for the Advisory community.

Grade Eight

At this age, students can be excited one minute and bored the next, highly motivated and then discouraged. Helping them see themselves as capable, productive people can go a long way toward keeping their motivation going.

This age group can exert a lot of peer pressure on others while simultaneously feeling peer pressure more strongly themselves. Guide them as they consider different sides of an issue and multiple solutions, and help them connect their natural interest in social justice to the conflicts and issues in their own lives.

Eighth graders are often sensitive and may take criticism personally. Make a point to emphasize the difference between critique of academic work, which has the goal of helping the student improve, and personal criticism.

Empathy

Explore how empathy can be put into action to create a safer school environment

---

Skills Practiced This Week

Asking/answering questions

Empathy

Helping others

Responsibility

Teamwork

DAY 1 ■ Developing Empathy

Arrival Welcome

Greet each student by name as they enter. Remind students to read the announcements message.

Announcements

> Welcome, Advisory Team!
>
> The Dalai Lama says, "Love and compassion are necessities, not luxuries. Without them, humanity cannot survive."
>
> Today you'll discuss a synonym for compassion: empathy. To have empathy means to be able to imagine yourself in another person's situation and understand what they're feeling.
>
> List ways someone has shown empathy toward you—at home, at school, or in the community.

Include upcoming school and team events in your messages this week.

Acknowledgments

Mix and Mingle Students walk around the room, greeting each other by name and offering a handshake or another friendly gesture. With each person they greet, they exchange one idea from their list. After students have talked to three or four classmates, ask a few volunteers to share one idea they heard that they connect with.

Activity

Mirrors Students stand, facing a partner, and decide who will lead first and who will follow. The leader begins by making slow and steady motions—without speaking—while the follower mirrors the movements. After 15–30 seconds, ring the chime (or use some other soothing sound). Students switch roles. Repeat as time allows.

Reflection "What are some ideas you heard about empathy that you connect to? What does it feel like when others show empathy to you? How might showing empathy make school a safer place?"

DAY 2 ■ Empathy in Action

Arrival Welcome

Greet each student by name as they enter. Encourage students to do a quick binder check as they get settled (see page 17).

Announcements

> Greetings, Brave Hearts!
>
> **Quote of the Day** "You must never be fearful about what you are doing when it is right." —ROSA PARKS, CIVIL RIGHTS ACTIVIST
>
> Yesterday you talked about empathy. Today you're going to explore putting empathy into action by supporting your peers at school (for example, avoiding gossip and including others at lunch).
>
> Think about how you support others at school. Be prepared to share your ideas with your table group.

Point out today's key school and team events.

Acknowledgments

Around-the-Table Chat Students greet their tablemates and then take turns sharing one idea about how they show empathy for others at school. Challenge each group to come up with as many ideas as possible and list them on paper. Post every group's list, and give students a few minutes to review them.

Activity

Hands Up for Empathy Post the words to this chant (see directions in margin). Students clap and chant the words together. One by one, going around the room, students insert one idea, such as "avoiding gossip," into the last line of the chant. Students continue clapping and repeating the last two lines, naming the next student, until everyone has had a turn.

Reflection Gather everyone in a circle. Ask: "What are three ways you're going to support others at school this week?"

Hands Up for Empathy Directions

"Hands up"
(put both hands up)

"For our team"
(clap, clap)

"Gonna name"
(clap, clap)

"Some peer support"
(clap, clap)

"One apiece"
(clap, clap)

"No repeats"
(clap, clap)

"No hesitation"
(clap, clap)

"No duplication"
(clap, clap)

"Starting with"
(clap, clap)

"[Student's name]"
(clap, clap)

_____ (student offers idea that fits the category)

(Pause)
(clap, clap)

Empathy

Explore how empathy can be put into action to create a safer school environment

DAY 3 ▪ A Safe, Positive School Climate

Arrival Welcome

Greet each student by name as they enter. Consider asking a few students "And how are you?" and listening attentively to their response.

Announcements

> Hey There, Community Builders!
>
> Think about this fact: About 30% of students in the United States have either bullied others or been a target of bullying; 70% of students have witnessed bullying.
>
> What can you do to promote a positive and safe school environment? Be ready to share your ideas.

Source for statistics: www.stopbullying.gov

Point out today's key school and team events.

Acknowledgments

Hey There Compliments In their table group, students greet each other by name and offer a compliment about how that student helps others. Give an example: "Hey there, Dana. You're always willing to help one of us if we get stuck on a math equation."

Activity

Consensus Mapping Give each group a Consensus Map.* Introduce the activity: "You're going to explore ways that you can promote a positive and safe school environment." Each student lists several ideas in one quadrant, and then students take turns reading their list to their group. Each student circles three ideas in their quadrant, and then nominates one of those ideas for consensus. If all members agree, they list this idea in their consensus circle, and continue until they have three to five items in their consensus circle. To extend the activity, try to reach a consensus as a whole group.

Reflection Gather everyone in a circle. Ask: "Think about the work you did this week around communication. How does kindness connect to communication? How can you communicate more kindness to others?"

*A Consensus Map template is available to download; see page 19.

DAY 4 ■ Are Your Questions and Comments Empathetic?

Arrival Welcome

Greet each student by name as they enter.

Announcements

> Hello, Team!
>
> In previous Advisories, you explored being respectful in how you talk and listen. To wrap up this week, you'll practice empathy in communication.
>
> If someone tells you some sad news, how can you communicate your empathy to them? Respond in writing or by drawing.

Point out today's (and/or this weekend's) key school and team events.

Acknowledgments

Word Splash In their table group, students greet each other by name and create a group Word Splash* using their words and drawings from the announcements prompt. Then each group presents and explains their Word Splash to the whole group. Display the Word Splashes where everyone can see them.

Activity

Empathy Role-Play Still with their table group, students role-play showing empathy when someone shares sad news with them (see guidelines at left). Circulate and coach as needed. Invite a few groups to share their role-play with the whole group.

Reflection "Looking back on this week, list three big ideas that you learned about empathy, two questions that you have about empathy, and one takeaway or practical tip that you plan to put into action."

*A Word Splash template and example are available to download; see page 19.

Role-Play Guidelines

➜ You or another adult should always take the part of anyone exhibiting negative behaviors, such as a student picking on others. (Having students act out negative behaviors can backfire by reinforcing those negative behaviors.)

➜ Prompt observers to notice the specific positive actions the actors demonstrate.

➜ Remind students to use respectful words and give positive feedback when debriefing.

Prioritize and De-stress

Develop strategies to de-stress and balance social and academic expectations with personal priorities

___

Skills Practiced This Week

___

Deep breathing/visualization

Managing stress

Organization

Perseverance

Teamwork

DAY 1 ▪ Coping With Stressors

Arrival Welcome

Greet each student by name as they enter. Remind students to read the announcements message.

Announcements

> Welcome Back, Advisory Team!
>
> A few years ago, Lady Gaga worked with Yale University on a research study. They asked high school students this question: "How do you currently feel in school?" "Tired" was the highest ranked response at 39%. "Stressed" came in second at 29%.
>
> Think about the students' responses above. Would one of them also be true for you? Why, or why not? Be ready to share.

Source for message: Yale Center for Emotional Intelligence, ei.yale.edu/what-we-do/emotion-revolution-student

Include upcoming school and team events in your messages this week.

Acknowledgments

What's the News? In their table group, one student begins by greeting the student to their left with "Good morning, _____. What's the news?" The student greeted responds with "Good morning, _____. The news is [student shares their response to the announcement prompt]." Continue around the table until all students have been greeted and have shared.

Activity

Maître d' Call out a table grouping (for example: "Table for 3!"). Students quickly form standing groups of that number. Pose a question about stressors for them to discuss (see examples in margin). Repeat as time allows, continuing to vary the table size.

Reflection "Not all stress is bad or harmful. For example, feeling stress before a race might motivate you to run your best. What are other examples of positive stressors? What can you do during the school day if you're feeling stressed? What are some things you can do in your free time to help you relax?"

Maître d' Examples

➤ **Table for 2:** What times of day do you feel most stressed, and why?

➤ **Table for 4:** How do you manage stress?

➤ **Table for 3:** Who might you talk to when you're feeling stressed?

DAY 2 ■ What's on Your Priorities List?

Arrival Welcome

Greet each student by name as they enter.

Announcements

> Greetings, Prioritizers!
>
> What's on your list of priorities?
>
> **Quote of the Day** "The key is not to prioritize what's on your schedule, but to schedule your priorities." —STEPHEN COVEY, AUTHOR, EDUCATOR
>
> On a sticky note, write down one thing that's a priority for you at school and one thing that's a personal priority. Be ready to share your ideas.

Point out today's key school and team events.

Acknowledgments

One-Minute Greeting Students greet as many people with a high five as they can in a minute. Then they form groups of four and take turns sharing their response to the announcements prompt. Collect everyone's sticky note for use tomorrow.

Activity

Graffiti Post chart paper around the room with the headings shown at left. Students "graffiti" their ideas on the chart (starting at any chart, going in any order, writing in any style anywhere on the chart). Assign small groups to find common themes and trends among the ideas on each chart. Each group shares a summary of their findings with the whole group. Post the completed charts for reference this week.

Graffiti Headings

➡ You have a day off from school. What do you do?

➡ You have a big test coming up. What do you do to prepare?

➡ What kind of music do you play to relax?

➡ How can you take care of your priorities this week?

Reflection "What are three things you can do this week that support your school priorities? Your personal priorities?"

Prioritize and De-stress

Develop strategies to de-stress and balance social and academic expectations with personal priorities

---

DAY 3 ▪ Finding a Balance

Arrival Welcome

Greet each student by name as they enter. Encourage students to do a quick binder check as they get settled (see page 17).

Announcements

Hello, Balancers!

You've been focused this week on balancing the academic pressures of middle school with other priorities in life. Think about a tip or strategy you keep in mind when balancing your own priorities.

Take a look back at the Graffiti charts and your priorities list from yesterday, and make note of what stands out to you.

Point out today's key school and team events.

Acknowledgments

What's Your Advice? One student in each table group begins by greeting the student to their left: "Good morning, Ollie. What's your advice about setting priorities [or managing stress]?" The student greeted responds: "Good morning, Toni. To manage stress, the advice I'd give is to get assignments in on time." Continue around the table until all students have shared.

Activity

Picture This Have students close their eyes and take a deep breath. Guide them through the visualization: "Think about something you really like doing. It could be listening to music, hanging out with a friend, anything that makes you feel peaceful and less stressed . . . Imagine yourself doing this activity. What do you see? . . . What do you hear? . . . What do you feel? . . . Now imagine that it's time to end the activity. As you do, you feel calm and relaxed." Give students a few moments to end their visualizations; then say, "On three, open your eyes. One, two, three." As time allows, ask volunteers to share what they visualized.

Reflection "How can visualization help you successfully meet a challenge, such as doing well on a test? Performing in front of people? Taking part in a sport?"

DAY 4 ■ Reducing Stress Schoolwide

Arrival Welcome

Greet each student by name as they enter. Consider also shaking hands.

Announcements

> Hi, Team!
>
> You've talked about priorities, stress, and finding a healthy balance for yourself. Since stress is so high for all students this time of year, it's important to think about how to help others find balance, too.
>
> Partner with one of your tablemates and brainstorm ideas about how to help others at school de-stress (for example, by starting a study group).

Point out today's (and/or this weekend's) key school and team events.

TIP

Meeting One-on-One With Your Advisees

You can use this time to pair up with one advisee to get to know them better and continue to strengthen your relationship with them.

Acknowledgments

Hand Up, Pair Up Students find a partner from a different table group, give a high five, and take turns sharing one idea for how they like to de-stress. Repeat for three more rounds, with students partnering each time with someone from a different table group.

Activity

Consensus Mapping Give each table group a Consensus Map.* Introduce the activity: "You're going to explore ways that you can help everyone at school de-stress." Each student lists several ideas in one quadrant, and then students take turns reading their list to their group. Each student circles three ideas in their quadrant, and then nominates one of their circled ideas for consensus. If all members agree, they list this idea in their consensus circle. The activity ends when the group has three to five items in their consensus circle. To extend the activity, try to reach a consensus as a whole group.

Reflection "Looking back on this week, list three big ideas that you learned about prioritizing and de-stressing, two takeaways or practical tips about prioritizing or de-stressing that can be put into action for the whole school, and one question that you have about anything related to priorities or stress."

*A Consensus Map template is available to download; see page 19.

A Fresh Start

Brainstorm ways to overcome obstacles and stay motivated to begin a new semester or quarter with focus and intention

---

Skills Practiced This Week

Analyzing
Drawing conclusions
Perseverance
Self-motivation
Summarizing

NOTE If students give their previous quarter a rating of 1 or 2, be prepared to talk (privately) about why they gave this rating, and then help them establish a strategic plan to have a better new quarter, including asking others for help when needed.

DAY 1 ▪ A Fresh Start

Arrival Welcome

Greet each student by name as they enter. Remind students to read the announcements message.

Announcements

> Welcome Back, Sensational Students!
>
> We're about to begin a new quarter. There's a lot to look forward to, but first, let's take a step back.
>
> Rate your previous quarter experience on a scale of 1 to 4 (1—ugh; 2—just OK; 3—very good; 4—great!). Be ready to share your rating and why you chose it.

Include upcoming school and team events in your messages this week.

Acknowledgments

Rating Our Previous Quarter Students pair up with a tablemate, greet their partner by name, and share their response to the announcements prompt. Each table group figures out their group's average rating and lists that rating on a chart or whiteboard so that the whole group can figure out the whole-group average.

Activity

I've Never . . . Explain that no matter how they rated the previous quarter, students can have a positive experience in the next quarter by trying something new. Pose this statement: "I've never _____, but I hope to in the next nine weeks." Students mix and mingle, partner up, and take turns sharing their completed statement. Repeat for several rounds, with students finding different partners each time.

Reflection "Think about what motivates you. If your previous quarter rating was 1 or 2, what might help you prime yourself for a better quarter next time? If your rating was 3 or 4, what could you do to help share that energy with others?"

DAY 2 ■ Bouncing Back From Setbacks

Arrival Welcome

As students enter, greet each one by name and model a friendly tone and body language.

Announcements

> Namaste, Advisory Team!
>
> **Quote of the Day** "There are no mistakes, save one: the failure to learn from a mistake." —ROBERT FRIPP, MUSICIAN
>
> Think about some mistakes you've read about (in a novel, perhaps), heard about (from a relative), or seen (on TV or in a movie). What can be learned from these mistakes? Be ready to share with your table group.

Point out today's key school and team events.

Acknowledgments

Around-the-Table Talk Round 1: Going in turn, each student greets their table-mates and briefly describes one mistake in response to the announcements prompt. Round 2: Going in turn, students briefly explain the lessons learned from the mistake they shared. Repeat both rounds as time allows. Ask a volunteer from each table group to summarize the lessons learned.

Activity

Maître d' Call out a table grouping (for example: "Table for 3!"). Students quickly form new groups of that number. Ask a question for them to discuss related to mistakes and lessons learned (see examples in margin). Give students 2–3 minutes to share. (Try to take part in some of the conversations as well.) Then call out a different table grouping, have students form new groups, and ask the same question or a new one. Repeat as time allows, continuing to vary the table size.

Maître d' Examples

➡ **Table for 4:** What's one positive thing you would do after making a mistake, and why?

➡ **Table for 3:** What can you do to avoid being too hard on yourself for making a mistake?

➡ **Table for 2:** What can you do to avoid making the same mistake twice?

Reflection "Write a summary of what you think you can learn from mistakes. Then list three concrete actions you plan to do the next time you make a mistake."

A Fresh Start

Brainstorm ways to overcome obstacles and stay motivated to begin a new semester or quarter with focus and intention

DAY 3 ▪ Getting Gritty

Arrival Welcome

Greet each student by name as they enter.

Announcements

Hey There, Grit Masters!

Quote of the Day "My character in [the movie] *True Grit* would set these goals for herself that seemed near impossible, but to her they were possible. She was never going to believe anything else other than that." —HAILEE STEINFELD, ACTRESS

To have grit means to have the strength and determination to push through challenges. How might people build grit? Be ready to share your thoughts with your table group.

Point out today's key school and team events.

Acknowledgments

Compliment Greetings With their table group, students greet each other by name and offer a compliment about a specific way that student has shown grit. Then as a group, students discuss their responses to the announcements prompt. Each group shares one of their ideas with the whole group.

Activity

Consensus Mapping Give each group a Consensus Map.* Introduce the activity: "You're going to explore ways that you can build grit, or get better at sticking with something new or challenging." Each student lists several ideas in one quadrant, and then students take turns reading their list to their group. Each student circles three ideas in their quadrant and then nominates one of those ideas for consensus. If all members agree, they list this idea in their consensus circle, and continue until they have three to five items in their consensus circle.

Reflection "What made reaching consensus successful? Did you encounter any hurdles? If so, how did you leap over them—was any 'grit' involved?"

*A Consensus Map template is available to download; see page 19.

DAY 4 ■ What *Really* Motivates You?

Arrival Welcome

As students enter, greet each one by name and ask: "How's your motivation for today—thumbs up, down, or in the middle?"

Announcements

Hello, Team!

Quote of the Day "To succeed, you need to find something to hold on to, something to motivate you, something to inspire you." —TONY DORSETT, COLLEGE AND PRO FOOTBALL HALL OF FAMER

List 3 to 5 things that motivate you—that inspire you to do your best and give your all. Also list 3 to 5 things that disrupt your motivation.

Point out today's (and/or this weekend's) key school and team events.

Acknowledgments

Group Brainstorm Going clockwise around the table, students greet each other by name and share their motivation disrupters (for example, negative comments). Going counterclockwise, students share what motivates them (for example, encouraging feedback). Then as a group, students agree on their top five disrupters and top five motivators. Each group shares their top five disrupters and motivators with the whole group.

Activity

Four Corners Pose one of the examples about motivation listed in the margin (or one you create), and designate one corner of the room for each response. Give students time to think about their choice (or the option that is closest to their choice). Then have them move to the corner of their choice and discuss why they chose it with a partner or small group there. Repeat for one or two more examples and responses as time allows.

Reflection "Looking back on this week, list three big ideas that you learned about grit and motivation, two questions that you have about grit and motivation, and one takeaway or practical tip about grit or motivation that you plan to put into action next week."

Four Corners Examples

➜ **I'm least inspired by**
1: Pressure my family puts on me
2: Pressure my teachers/coaches put on me
3: Pressure I put on myself
4: Pressure my friends put on me

➜ **I'm most inspired by**
1: My family
2: My teachers/coaches
3: Myself
4: My friends

➜ **I stay motivated by**
1: Talking with my family
2: Talking with my teachers/coaches
3: Self-talk/self-reflection
4: Talking with my friends

Reflecting and Envisioning

Reflect on recently met goals and Advisory experiences to identify skills that can help with future achievements

Skills Practiced This Week

Cooperation
Goal-setting
Self-control
Self-reflection

Just Like Me Prompt Ideas

➜ A key to my success was having a positive attitude.

➜ Making to-do lists and prioritizing them helped me meet project deadlines.

➜ When I need to refocus, I take an ice cream break.

DAY 1 ▪ Revisiting Our Goals

Arrival Welcome

Greet each student by name as they enter. Remind students to read the announcements message.

Announcements

> Welcome, Progress Makers!
>
> The end of the 2nd quarter is near. It's time to review your SMART goal(s) and check on your progress. And if you've already reached your goal(s), congrats! Now's a great time to set some new goals.
>
> Take a SMART goal sheet. Think about your successes this quarter, big and small. What were some keys to your success? (For example: being more organized; asking for extra help.) On sticky notes, list 3 to 5 keys to success, and be prepared to share them.

Include upcoming school and team events in your messages this week.

Acknowledgments

What's the News? In their table group, one student begins by greeting the student to their left by saying "Good morning, _____. What's the news?" The student greeted responds with "Good morning, _____. The news is [student shares their response to the announcements prompt]." Continue around the table until all students have been greeted and have shared. Collect everyone's SMART goal* sheet for use in a future Advisory.

Activity

Just Like Me Use ideas from students' sticky notes as prompts. As you say each prompt, students who feel it applies to them stand up (or raise hands if standing is difficult) and say "Just like me" at the same time. Take time to observe who does not stand up (or who doesn't stand as often), and check in with them to to help them dig deeper into their goals for keys to success. Repeat for as many rounds as time allows.

Reflection "Just for yourself: List recent successes. Bring this list home with you, and before you go to sleep, read it and let yourself dream of future success!"

*A SMART goal template is available to download; see page 19.

DAY 2 ▪ Strengthening Academic Skills

Arrival Welcome

Greet each student by name as they enter. Encourage students to do a quick binder check as they get settled (see page 17).

Announcements

Hi, Middle School Mentors!

A mentor is an experienced guide or coach—someone you can confide in and turn to for advice. My mentor was Ms. Nash. She coached and guided me during my first year of teaching and made a big difference in my career.

If you were a mentor for a student about to start middle school, what advice would you give about how to be academically successful? Be ready to share.

Point out today's key school and team events.

Acknowledgments

What's Your Advice? One student in each table group begins by greeting the student to their left with "Good morning, _____. What's your advice?" That student returns the greeting and shares their advice. Continue around the table for two to three rounds. Then have a few students summarize their group's ideas and share them with the whole group.

Activity

Number Freeze Everyone begins sitting. Call out a target number—less than the total number of students but more than one-third the number. (For example, for 17 students, pick a number between 6 and 16.) Set a timer for 60 seconds and say "Go!" Students try to get the target number of people to stand at the same time, following these rules: No one may talk or point; anyone may stand at any time, but not for more than 5 seconds at a time (students count to 5 silently). When you think the target number has been reached (or when the timer goes off), say "Freeze!" Students stay in position while you count those standing to see if the numbers match. Repeat with a new number.

Reflection "List some of the academic skills and strategies you learned today that you'd like to work on. How will you benefit by working on these?"

Reflecting and Envisioning

Reflect on recently met goals and Advisory experiences to identify skills that can help with future achievements

DAY 3 ■ A Look Back, a Look Ahead

Arrival Welcome

Greet each student by name as they enter.

Announcements

Hello, Reflective Thinkers!

Quote of the Day "Life can only be understood backwards; but it must be lived forwards." —SØREN KIERKEGAARD, PHILOSOPHER, AUTHOR

Think about what this quote means to you, and then write down your thoughts.

Point out today's key school and team events.

Acknowledgments

Around-the-Table Talk In their table group, students greet each other by name with "Good morning!" and take turns sharing their responses to the announcements prompt. Then they describe one academic experience that could have had better results, what they learned from it, and how it helped them move forward. (For example: "I almost flunked a test. I thought the class was easy, so I spaced out a lot. From that experience, I learned to pay attention to everything that goes on in class!") Ask a few volunteers to share their experiences with the whole group.

Activity

Snowball Students write an anonymous response to this prompt on a piece of paper: "If you throw a stone into a puddle or a lake, ripples move across the water long after the stone is thrown. How do you think Advisory meetings have created a ripple effect in our classroom community?" Then they form a circle, crumple their paper into a "snowball," and toss it gently into the center. Students pick up one snowball near them and read aloud what's on the paper.

Reflection "What have you learned about yourself from our Advisory meetings? What have you learned about your classmates? How does this knowledge help you move forward in your thinking?"

DAY 4 ■ The Joy of Compliments

Arrival Welcome

Greet each student by name as they enter. Consider also giving a sincere compliment.

Announcements

> Congrats, Advisory Team!
>
> You have all been working really hard at building positive relationships in Advisory and learning how to communicate better. Today we will join those two things together by practicing giving compliments.
>
> Take a minute to think about specific ways your tablemates work together or help one another. Be ready to share compliments with your tablemates.

Point out today's (and/or this weekend's) key school and team events.

Acknowledgments

Compliment Greeting In their table group, students greet each other by name and offer a specific compliment about the person's helpful actions. Be clear that the compliment should be about the person's actions, not their appearance. Each group then shares one of their group's ideas with the whole group.

Activity

The Last Word Have students form small groups, give each group chart paper, and assign roles: recorder and presenter. Explain that students will write the word "Advisory" on their paper and brainstorm words or phrases related to Advisory that start with each letter of the word. Ask presenters to share one of their group's words or phrases and its connection to Advisory with the whole group. Write these on chart paper or a whiteboard. After each group has shared, open up discussion to include related words or phrases that weren't listed.

Reflection "List three big ideas you learned about yourself or your Advisory team-mates this semester; two practical tips that we can use to improve Advisory for next semester; and one question you have about anything related to Advisory, school, or life."

The Last Word Example

Advice

Discussions

Viewpoints

Insights

Significant

Opinions welcome!

Respectful

Yourself (you can be yourself in Advisory!)

Teamwork and Team Spirit

Reflect on independent leadership projects to plan for future successes

---

Skills Practiced This Week

Evaluating
Making connections
Self-control
Self-reflection
Teamwork

NOTE Return each group's Advisory plan. Students will share what they learned from the "Student-Led Advisory Planning" and Student-Led Advisory Week" Advisory weeks on pages 92–99.

DAY 1 ▪ You've Gone on a Mission

Arrival Welcome

Greet each student by name as they enter. Remind students to read the announcements message.

Announcements

> Welcome, Mission Control!
>
> Think of your Student-Led Advisory as a mission that you've all gone on. Now that the mission's complete and you've had some time away from it, you're going to evaluate what went well, what could be improved upon for next time, and some of your "mission" favorites.
>
> What is something that really stuck with you from your Student-Led Advisory (either in planning or leading)? Be ready to share with a partner.

Include upcoming school and team events in your messages this week.

Acknowledgments

Partner Chat Students pair up, greet each other, and share their ideas in response to the announcements prompt. Ask a few volunteers to share one of the ideas they discussed with the whole group.

Activity

Ball Toss Use any kind of squishy ball or beach ball. Students stand by their desks or in a circle. Call out a student's name and gently toss the ball under-hand to that student, who then shares a favorite part of the Student-Led Advisory, and why. For example: "My favorite part was when my group brainstormed which activity to do for our Advisory because it made me emember all the fun activities we did this year." Then the student calls out another student's name, tosses the ball to that student, and sits down or crosses arms. Repeat until everyone has had a turn.

Reflection Gather everyone in a circle. Ask: "Why do you think it's important to reflect on and evaluate a project, presentation, or other lesson you've recently completed?"

DAY 2 ■ Debriefing the Mission

Arrival Welcome

Greet each student by name as they enter.

Announcements

> Hi, Team!
>
> Today you're going to debrief your group's Student-Led Advisory from a couple of weeks ago. Remember to focus on actions, not people.
>
> Think of your Advisory day (planning and leading). Jot down a list of things that went well and a list of things that could have gone more smoothly. Be ready to share with your group.

Point out today's key school and team events.

Acknowledgments

Group Sharing Students gather in their Student-Led Advisory group, greet each other by name, and take turns sharing "things that went well" from the announcements prompt. Then they have a more free-flowing discussion about why these things went well. Students stay in their group.

Activity

Consensus Mapping (variation) Give each group chart paper and designate a recorder in each group. The recorder makes a circle in the middle of the chart paper and labels it "Consensus." Each student shares their "could have gone more smoothly" list from the announcements prompt. Then they circle their top three ideas and nominate one of these for consensus. If all members agree, the recorder lists the idea on the chart paper (not in the circle). Then the group chooses their top three to five ideas. The recorder lists these in the consensus circle. Each group shares one of their ideas with the whole group.

Reflection "What did you learn from your debrief? How might you do things differently next time? What would you do the same? Why?"

Teamwork and Team Spirit

Reflect on independent leadership projects to plan for future successes

---

DAY 3 ■ Preparing for the Future

Arrival Welcome

Greet each student by name as they enter. Encourage students to do a quick binder check as they get settled (see page 17).

Announcements

> Hello, Commanders!
>
> Now that you've debriefed your Student-Led Advisory, you're going to think about future missions.
>
> **Quote of the Day** "If you know whence you came, there are absolutely no limitations to where you can go." —JAMES BALDWIN, AUTHOR, POET
>
> What does the Quote of the Day mean to you? How might it apply to future projects similar to your Student-Led Advisory? Be ready to share your ideas.

Point out today's key school and team events.

TIP

Meeting One-on-One With Your Advisees

You can use this time to pair up with one advisee to get to know them better and continue to strengthen your relationship with them.

Acknowledgments

Mix and Mingle Students walk around the room and greet someone nearby by name. Then they exchange their responses to the announcements prompt. After students have talked with three to four classmates, ask a few volunteers to share something they heard that they connected to.

Activity

Ball Toss Use any kind of squishy ball or beach ball. Students stand at their desks or in a circle. Ask: "What are you most proud of in your planning and leading of your Advisory?" and toss the ball to a student. The student who catches the ball shares their response, tosses the ball to someone else, and sits down. Continue until everyone has had a chance to respond. Do more rounds as time allows, asking different questions. For example: "What is one piece of advice you would give someone about planning and leading an Advisory?"

Reflection Gather everyone in a circle. Ask: "How does debriefing make you a better learner? A better leader? A better team player?"

DAY 4 ■ Celebrating Successes

Arrival Welcome

Greet each student by name as they enter. Consider also giving a handshake.

Announcements

> Congrats, Advisory Team!
>
> You've successfully completed your mission debrief and are more than ready for future missions, wherever they may take you.
>
> What made your teamwork this week successful? Be ready to share.

Point out today's (and/or this weekend's) key school and team events.

Acknowledgments

Hand Up, Pair Up Students walk around the room with one hand up. When they find a partner, they greet each other by name, give a high five, and share their thoughts on the announcements prompt. Students greet at least five different classmates. Invite a few volunteers to share one thing they heard that they connected to.

Activity

Body Drumming Have students stand and spread out so that they have enough room to do the motions safely. First teach and practice a three-count stomp-and-clap pattern: Stomp, stomp, clap! Stomp, stomp, clap! Then teach and practice a four-count pattern: Stomp, stomp, stomp, clap! Stomp, stomp, stomp, clap!

Divide the class in half and assign one half the three-count pattern and the other half the four-count pattern. On your signal, the two groups perform their pattern simultaneously. After 1–2 minutes, signal for all students to stop at the same time. Repeat.

To add challenge, create more elaborate drumming patterns.

Reflection Gather everyone in a circle. Ask: "The last week of school is approaching. What can you do to reinforce teamwork during the last days of school? What are you looking forward to most next week?"

Extend Learning Through Themes

4-Day Plans

Tips for Extending Learning Through Themes

All Grades

Students will learn a lot about each other over the school year. To build on these connections, encourage students to take action on what they have in common, perhaps starting a book club, hobby group, or other club based on their shared interests.

Many middle school students will be ready to take on more of a leadership role. Cross-age tutoring and peer mediation offer opportunities for students in different grades to work together productively. Students may also be ready to care for or read to younger children, or to organize service projects for the wider community.

In general, connecting the activities of Advisory to the larger world will help students see the relevance of what they're learning and practicing. It will also help students begin to visualize possibilities for their own futures as they try out new interests.

Grade Six

Students may be especially interested in sports and outdoor activities, particularly team sports. Incorporate energetic team activities into Advisory to keep students energized. Also, encourage them to build connections and stay engaged in school by joining existing after-school activities or teams or starting new ones, such as disc golf or hiking.

As they grow more able to see the world from varied points of view, sixth graders may enjoy learning about different cultures from around the world. They also like learning about older and younger people, so give them opportunities to read, learn, and talk to and about people from various backgrounds.

Sixth graders may also start to take an interest in languages, music, or mechanics. Find ways to incorporate these natural areas of interest into Advisory to help students build on budding skills.

Grade Seven

Seventh graders are often trying out new interests, so give them the opportunity to explore a variety of pursuits. These students also have strong leadership skills, so allow them the chance to take on a leading role during Advisory activities.

Some seventh graders may be struggling to establish their own identity and fit in with a positive peer group. Belonging to a school or community group, such as one that tutors younger students or helps families in the community, can help students define themselves in a positive way and develop a sense of purpose.

Students at this age are often interested in both getting jobs to make money and serving the community. Use these interests to encourage social entrepreneurialism and fundraising for causes that students believe in.

Grade Eight

At this age, students are naturally interested in problems in the wider world and eager to find solutions. Take time to discuss ways in which they can help create change within their school, their community, and the wider world.

These students may already have experience with volunteering and making connections within the larger community. Encourage them to brainstorm ways they can become more involved in the service roles they already hold and foster school-community connections through these roles.

Leverage this age group's interest in current events to make connections to bullying prevention and victim advocacy in a broader context. Help them see the "current events" in their own lives and in the larger school community, and guide them to apply their sense of social justice when interacting on a personal level.

Our Common Interests

Foster community by planning activities based on common interests

---

Skills Practiced This Week

Building community
Making connections
Organization
Persuading others
Teamwork

DAY 1 ▪ Revisiting Our Favorites

Arrival Welcome

Greet each student by name as they enter. Remind them to read the announcements message.

Announcements

> Welcome, Advisory Team!
>
> Since the first week of school, you've learned a lot about each other. But likes and dislikes can change over time. Let's see what's changed (or stayed the same)!
>
> Write your responses to the following questions: What's your favorite food? Favorite show/movie? Favorite sport, game, or activity? Have any of your responses changed since you answered these same questions at the beginning of the year?

Include upcoming school and team events in your messages this week.

Acknowledgments

Partner Chat In their table group, students greet each other by name. With a partner, they take turns sharing their responses to each "favorite" question from the announcements prompt. Then students talk as a group about whether any of their responses have changed since the beginning of the year, and if so, why.

Activity

Fact or Fiction Students write three statements about themselves: two are factual (true); one is fictional (false). For example: "I love anchovy pizza [T]. My favorite book genre is science fiction [T]. I like to play video games [F]." Choose the first student to read their statements. The other students vote on which statement they think is false. Then the reader reveals the false one. Continue until everyone has shared, or spread this activity over several Advisory meetings.

Reflection Have students pair up with someone who has similar favorites/interests to briefly discuss their reasons why these are their favorites.

DAY 2 ▪ Activity Wish List

Arrival Welcome

Greet each student by name as they enter. Check in with a few students about how they're doing with staying on top of their assignments.

Announcements

Hello, Team!

Think about every activity you do after school and on weekends. Pause for a moment. Now think about new activities you'd like to try—maybe a new sport (disc golf), hobby (3D drawing), or club (book group, recycling team).

List your top 3 after-school/weekend activities (ones you do now) and then make a wish list of the top 3 new activities you'd like to try.

Point out today's key school and team events.

Acknowledgments

Around-the-Table Talk After students greet their tablemates, they take turns sharing their response to the announcements prompt. Going counterclockwise, students share their top three current activities. Going clockwise, they share the activities on their wish list.

Activity

Common Commonalities Introduce the topic: "If new activities were to be offered at school, which ones would you want to see offered?" Students pair up to brainstorm and list ideas. Then each pair joins another pair to share ideas. The group circles the ideas that all four group members would like to see offered, and a spokesperson from each group shares their commonalities with the whole group. List these on chart paper or a whiteboard. (Save this list for students to reference the rest of the week.)

Reflection "What strategies did you use to find commonalities?"

Our Common Interests

Foster community by planning activities based on common interests

DAY 3 ▪ Activity Action Plan, PART 1

Arrival Welcome

Greet each student by name as they enter. Check in with a few more students about how they're doing with staying on top of their assignments.

Announcements

Dear Activity Proponents,

Today we're going to keep talking about school activities. Although we don't know if we can actually add more activities, we can try to make this happen. We'll start by doing some early planning together.

Look over the Common Commonalities list you created yesterday. Which 2 or 3 ideas for activities interest you the most? Take a few minutes to think about your choices.

Point out today's key school and team events.

Acknowledgments

Snowball Students write down their anonymous response to the announcements prompt on a piece of paper and crumple it into a "snowball." Then they form a circle and gently toss their snowball into the center. Students pick up one snowball near them, pair up, and share what's on their paper. While they talk, roam and record some ideas you hear.

Activity

Action Plan, Part 1 Staying in the same pairs, students choose one of the activity ideas from their snowballs. Then they discuss and record their responses to these questions: (1) What types of learning or skills would students gain from this activity? (2) What resources or equipment would the activity need? (3) Why is offering this activity at school a good idea? Collect everyone's responses, and as time allows, invite pairs to share their responses to question #3.

Reflection Gather everyone in a circle. Ask: "How would your proposed activity positively affect our school?"

DAY 4 ■ Activity Action Plan, PART 2

Arrival Welcome

Greet each student by name as they enter.

Announcements

> Hello Again, Activity Proponents!
>
> As we wrap up our planning, think about the art of persuasion: Communicating ideas effectively so that your point of view is understood—and maybe even convincing others to take action.
>
> What might you say and do to persuade [insert school principal's name] to consider adding an activity you're interested in? Be ready to share your ideas.

Point out today's (and/or this weekend's) key school and team events.

Acknowledgments

Maître d' Call out a table grouping (for example: "Table for 3!"). Students quickly form groups of that number. Pose a question for them to discuss (see examples in margin). Give students 1–2 minutes to share. Repeat as time allows, continuing to vary the table size.

Activity

Action Plan, Part 2 In pairs or small groups, students choose which activity they want to draft a plan for to present to the principal (based on the Maître d' question responses). They'll also need to decide how to present their action plan (for example, via a letter or email, or in person). During future Advisories, students can finalize their plans and decide on next steps with you.

Reflection Gather everyone in a circle. Ask: "How well did you work together today, and why? What are your next steps?" Have students discuss with their partner or group.

Maître d' Examples

→ **Table for 2:** What are some questions the principal might ask about your activity ideas?

→ **Table for 3:** When could these activities be scheduled? Consider the time needed for other school events and activities.

→ **Table for 4:** What would you say if the principal asks how our school would benefit from these activities?

→ **Table for 3:** Which adults at school could help run these activities, and why?

Safety for One and All

Gain a better understanding of the importance of safety and learn how to support safety for all in school

Skills Practiced This Week

Assertiveness
Building community
Cooperation
Helping others
Inferring/interpreting

DAY 1 ▪ Safety First!

Arrival Welcome

Greet each student by name as they enter. Remind students to read the announcements message.

Announcements

Hello, Advisory Team!

Today we're starting a conversation about safety at school. Think about what the word "safe" means to you.

Write your personal definition of the word "safe" on a slip of paper (for example, "I feel safe when . . ." or "Being safe means . . .").

Include upcoming school and team events in your messages this week.

Acknowledgments

Around-the-Table Talk Going clockwise, students send a "hello" and a high five around their table group. Going counterclockwise, students share their personal definitions of "safe." Going clockwise, students think about places where they feel safe and share one place with their group.

Activity

Word Splash Use chart paper or a whiteboard to create a whole-group Word Splash* about the word "safe." Choose a recorder, and allow a minute for silent brainstorming. Then guide the whole group in brainstorming out loud (remind students that there are no right or wrong ideas in brainstorming). After everyone's ideas are written down, invite students to share what they notice about the completed Word Splash. The recorder adds new ideas that arise from this sharing. Post the Word Splash for future reference.

Reflection Gather students in a circle. Ask: "How could we as a whole group define 'safe' now? Based on our Word Splash and discussions, how important do you think it is to feel safe at school, and why?"

*A Word Splash template and example are available to download; see page 19.

DAY 2 ■ When We Don't Feel Safe

Arrival Welcome

As students enter, greet each one by name, and model a friendly tone and body language.

Announcements

Welcome, Team!

Take a look again at our Word Splash from yesterday. Our school is a safe place overall, but we can always do more to promote school safety.

Take an index card and list 3 concerns you have about safety (at school, in the neighborhood, or on social media). Do not write your name on your card. Fold it in half when you're done.

Point out today's key school and team events.

Acknowledgments

Info Exchange Students mix and mingle, greeting each other by name and giving high fives. On your signal, they stop, form pairs, and exchange cards without looking at them. Do two more exchanges in this way to ensure that all cards are anonymous. On your next signal, students form pairs and discuss what's on the cards they're holding. Finally, students exchange cards with their partner one last time and return to their table groups.

Activity

Analyzing Data In their table group, students share the information on their Info Exchange cards. Then they determine their top three concerns from the ones listed on their cards. Each group reports those top three concerns to the whole group. List these on chart paper or a whiteboard, or have a volunteer do so. Determine the whole group's top three concerns by noting repeated concerns and voting if necessary. Students will use these results in tomorrow's Advisory.

Reflection "What's one thing that stands out to you about our whole group's concerns?"

Safety for One and All

Gain a better understanding of the importance of safety and learn how to support safety for all in school

---

Carousel Examples

➔ **Concern 1: Cyberbullying**
"Think before you post."

➔ **Concern 2: Cliques**
"Include everyone."

➔ **Concern 3: Gossip**
"Walk away."

➔ **Our School Climate**
"Treat everyone with respect."

➔ **Our Community**
"Walk with a friend."

➔ **Our World**
"Support or join a global cause."

DAY 3 ■ # Making Our School Even Safer

Arrival Welcome

Greet each student by name as they enter.

Announcements

Hello, Thoughtful Thinkers,

Quote of the Day "It's easy to hate. It takes strength to be gentle and kind." —STEVEN PATRICK MORRISSEY, MUSICIAN

Think about our discussions this week about safety. With a partner, chat about how you think this quote connects to making our school and community safer for everyone.

Point out today's key school and team events.

Acknowledgments

One-Sentence Sharing Students count off to form groups of four. They greet each other by name and take turns sharing one sentence about what they can do to help classmates feel safer. For example: "We can use a respectful tone and kind words when we talk to each other." Give students 30 seconds of think time before they begin sharing ideas.

Activity

Carousel Explain that in this activity students will be thinking more about their top three concerns from the previous day. Post six pieces of chart paper around the room, each with a label shown at left (or similar ones). Give each group a different colored marker. With each group starting out at a different chart, students brainstorm ideas for positive ways to address the chart's topic and record them on the chart (examples at left). On your signal, groups rotate to the next chart and add to the listed ideas. Conclude once all groups have visited every chart.

Reflection Gather everyone in a circle. Ask: "Look at all the ideas you generated! Now the real work begins. What might be a challenge when putting these ideas into action?"

DAY 4 ▪ Public Safety Announcement

Arrival Welcome

As students enter, greet each one by name and ask: "How are your thinking skills for today—thumbs up, down, or in the middle?"

Announcements

Hi, Team!

Today you're going to explore how to handle—in positive ways—situations that might feel unsafe.

Chat quietly with a classmate about potentially unsafe situations. (Idea to prompt your thinking: being followed down the street while walking alone.)

Point out today's (and/or this weekend's) key school and team events.

Acknowledgments

Group Brainstorm In their table group, students greet each other and then brainstorm a list of unsafe situations someone might face. They then brainstorm a list of positive strategies for handling their unsafe situations. Students agree on their group's three most unsafe situations and top three positive strategies, and then take turns sharing them with the whole group. Post each group's top choices on chart paper or the class bulletin board for students' future reference.

Activity

Role-Play The goal of this role-play is to give students practice using positive strategies when faced with challenging situations. (See guidelines in margin.) As a whole group, choose a situation to role-play based on the acknowledgments discussions. Ask two or three students to serve as actors with you (or another adult), and together privately plan your role-play. Have everyone else jot down ideas about how they'd handle the situation. Perform the role-play (3–5 minutes). Debrief as a whole group, focusing on positive strategies the students think worked. Invite a new group of students to role-play.

Reflection Gather everyone in a circle. Ask: "What made the performance fun and successful? How can you use what you learned today to support one another in reaching your goals?"

Role-Play Guidelines

➡ You or another adult should always take the part of anyone exhibiting negative behaviors, such as a student picking on others. (Having students act out negative behaviors can backfire by reinforcing those negative behaviors.)

➡ Prompt observers to notice the specific positive actions the actors demonstrate.

➡ Remind students to use respectful words and give positive feedback when debriefing.

Handling Stress

Identify stressors, and outline plans for managing them

Skills Practiced This Week

Empathy
Figurative thinking
Managing stress
Public speaking
Self-awareness

DAY 1 ■ Metaphorically Speaking: What Is Stress?

Arrival Welcome

Greet each student by name as they enter. Remind students to read the announcements message.

Announcements

Hello, Team!

This week, you're going to dig deeper into what causes stress and how you can better manage stress.

Quote of the Day "Stress is the trash of modern life—we all generate it but if you don't dispose of it properly, it will pile up and overtake your life." —DANZAE PACE, WRITER

The above quote uses trash as a metaphor for stress. What are some other metaphors (or similes) for stress? Take a sheet of paper and write down 2 or 3 metaphors/similes for stress. Be ready to share.

Include upcoming school and team events in your messages this week.

Acknowledgments

Swap Meet Students mix and mingle, greeting each other with a handshake or a high five. On your signal, students find a partner close to them and share their lists from the announcements prompt. Encourage students to record any of their partner's ideas that they connect with. Repeat for two to four more rounds. Collect everyone's list.

Activity

Museum Walk Display students' metaphors/similes around the room or on tables. Students walk around and review them and draw a star next to any ideas they connect with. Gather students together and invite volunteers to share their observations. Collect the lists again to generate an anchor chart for students to reference the rest of the week.

Reflection Gather everyone in a circle. Ask: "How do you think making connections like these might help someone who is experiencing stress?"

DAY 2 ■ Take a Step Back

Arrival Welcome

Greet each student by name as they enter. Consider adding in a handshake or high five.

Announcements

> Hi, Brainstormers!
>
> There are many factors that can contribute to stress. Some may be external (such as a traumatic event) and some may be internal (such as anxiety). While you can't control all factors that lead to stress, there are ways to manage them.
>
> Think of an external factor and an internal factor that might cause someone stress. Be ready to share.

Point out today's key school and team events.

Acknowledgments

Group Brainstorm In their table group, students greet each other and then brainstorm a list of external factors that can cause stress and a list of internal factors. Then they brainstorm positive strategies for responding to these factors.

Activity

Graffiti Post chart paper around the room with the headings shown at left. Students "graffiti" their ideas on the charts (starting at any chart, going in any order, writing in any style anywhere on the chart). Students then form small groups to review the completed charts. Each group stars which factors they think someone has control over (for example, being disorganized) and circles factors that are out of a person's control (for example, the death of a loved one). Each group summarizes their findings for the whole group. Keep the Graffiti charts up for the rest of the week.

Graffiti Headings

- ➔ Symptoms of Stress
- ➔ External Factors
- ➔ Internal Factors
- ➔ Positive Strategies

Reflection Gather everyone in a circle. Ask: "What is something you learned today? Looking at the Graffiti charts, which strategies do you think are the most important for a person handling external factors that may be out of their control?"

Handling Stress

Identify stressors and outline plans for managing them

DAY 3 ■ Finding Support

Arrival Welcome

Greet each student by name as they enter. Encourage students to do a quick binder check as they get settled (see page 17).

Announcements

> Hello, Supportive Team!
>
> Today you'll discuss helpful resources for someone who is experiencing stress.
>
> **Quote of the Day** "Ask for help, not because you are weak, but because you want to remain strong." —LES BROWN, AUTHOR, MOTIVATIONAL SPEAKER
>
> What does the above quote mean to you? Be ready to share.

Point out today's key school and team events.

Acknowledgments

Interview Students greet their table partner by name and take turns interviewing each other about (1) their response to the announcements prompt; (2) people in their lives they can go to for help when they need it; (3) adults at school they trust who could help them when they're dealing with stress.

Activity

Word Splash In their table group, students create a Word Splash* of people at their school and outside of school who could help them if they experience stress. Each group presents their World Splash to the whole group. Display the Word Splashes where everyone can see them. Students will reference these tomorrow.

Reflection Gather everyone in a circle. Ask: "What do you notice about everyone's Word Splashes? What similarities can you find?"

*A Word Splash template and example are available to download; see page 19.

DAY 4 ■ Just Breathe

Arrival Welcome

Greet each student by name as they enter. Consider playing quiet, relaxing music while students enter and respond to the announcements prompt.

Announcements

Hi, Team!

Quote of the Day "Sometimes the most important thing in a whole day is the rest we take in between two breaths." —ETTY HILLESUM, WRITER, VICTIM OF THE HOLOCAUST

Slowly breathe in; slowly breathe out. Then think about ways someone experiencing stress might find moments of peace (for example, by closing their eyes and listening to relaxing music or sounds). Be ready to share.

Point out today's (and/or this weekend's) key school and team events.

Acknowledgments

Around-the-Table Chat Assign a recorder for each table group. Students greet their tablemates by name and then take turns sharing their response to the announcements prompt. Then they have a free-flowing discussion to reach consensus on three to five ways to find moments of peace. The recorder writes these down. After a couple of minutes, have each group share their list. Write these on chart paper or a whiteboard.

Activity

Creating a Public Service Announcement (PSA) Working with their table group, students create a PSA (poster, radio ad, or TV ad) using what they've learned this week about stress. You may want to spread this activity over several Advisory meetings so that students have time to plan, draft, revise, and rehearse as needed. Each group displays or presents their PSA to the whole group, then to the whole school, and finally to the wider community.

Reflection On a piece of paper, students anonymously write the most important thing they learned about stress this week. Standing in a circle, they crumple up their paper into a "snowball" and gently toss it into the middle of the room. Then they pick up a nearby snowball and take turns reading them aloud.

> **TIP**
>
> **Meeting One-on-One With Your Advisees**
>
> You can use this time to pair up with one advisee to get to know them better and continue to strengthen your relationship with them.

Community Outreach

Strengthen community through the planning of a community service project

---

Skills Practiced This Week

Building community

Brainstorming

Organization

Speaking essentials

Just Like Me Prompt Ideas

→ I like to go to [Name] Park.

→ I have a savings account at a local bank.

→ My family picks out fresh vegetables at our local farm stand [or bodega or marketplace].

DAY 1 ▪ Community All Around Us

Arrival Welcome

Greet each student by name as they enter. Remind students to read the announcements message.

Announcements

Welcome, Community Members!

Our school community is part of the greater community that we live in.

Think of a business, an organization, a service provider, or an institution in our greater community that is important to you. Be ready to share your response and why it's important.

Include upcoming school and team events in your messages this week.

Acknowledgments

What's the News? In their table group, one student begins by greeting the student to their left with "Good morning, _____. What's the news?" The student greeted responds "Good morning, _____. The news is [student shares their response to the announcements prompt]." Continue around the table until all students have shared their responses. Invite a few volunteers to share one of their group's responses with the whole group.

Activity

Just Like Me Adapt what students shared during What's the News? to create prompts for topics. As you say each prompt, students who feel it applies to them stand up (or raise hands if standing is difficult) and say "Just like me" at the same time. Take time to observe who does not stand up (or doesn't stand up as often), and check in with them to hear their ideas. Repeat for as many rounds as time allows.

Reflection Gather everyone in a circle. Ask: "How do the people and places in our community strengthen our community as a whole?"

DAY 2 ▪ Community Connections

Arrival Welcome

Greet each student by name as they enter. Consider adding in a handshake or a high five.

Announcements

> Hi, Team!
>
> Today you're going to explore how we're all connected to people and places in our greater community.
>
> Take a card and read its word or phrase to yourself. Think about how you and other people in our community are connected to your word or phrase. Be ready to share.

Point out today's key school and team events.

Acknowledgments

Card Match Students walk around the room and greet each other by name until they find a match. Partners then discuss how the terms on their People and Places in Our Community cards* are interdependent. For example, if one student has "pet owner" and the other has "veterinarian," the pair can discuss how people who own pets depend on a veterinarian to take care of their pets; likewise, in order to make a living, a veterinarian depends on people who own pets. Have a few pairs share their ideas with the whole group. Students stay with their partners.

Activity

Common Commonalities Introduce the topic: "What are some ways that people can volunteer or help out in our community? For example: Someone might organize a neighborhood cleanup." Students pair up to brainstorm and list ideas. Then each pair joins another pair to share ideas. They circle the ideas all four group members want to try. A spokesperson from each group shares these with the whole group. List the ideas and post where everyone can see. Students will reference this list tomorrow.

Reflection "What strategies did you use to find commonalities?"

*People and Places in Our Community cards are available to download; see page 19.

Volunteering Ideas

➤ Research volunteer opportunities in your community that students could participate in.

➤ Invite people from the community to come talk to students about their volunteer efforts (or their organization) and how students could get involved.

➤ Reach out to the people running the places where students are interested in volunteering, and ask what types of volunteer help they might need.

Community Outreach

Strengthen community through the planning of a community service project

---

DAY 3 ■ Lend a Helping Hand

Arrival Welcome

Greet each student by name as they enter. Encourage students to do a quick binder check as they get settled (see page 17).

Announcements

> Hello, Community Volunteers!
>
> Yesterday you all came up with ways to help out in our community. Today you're going to create an action plan for one of those ideas.
>
> On our list from yesterday, put a star next to four volunteer ideas that you'd be interested in planning.

Point out today's key school and team events.

Acknowledgments

Four Corners (variation) As a whole group, tally up the stars to find the top four volunteer ideas. Circle these. Designate one corner of the room for each of the top four volunteer ideas. Give students some time to think about their choice (or the option that is closest to their choice). Students move to that corner, greet the students there by name, and share one reason why they made that choice.

Activity

Help-a-thon Action Plan, Part 1 Tell students they're going to plan a volunteer activity for their Four Corners choice. Give each group chart paper and have them label it "Help-a-thon" along with the name of their chosen activity. Each group discusses and records their responses to these questions: (1) What is the goal of your Help-a-thon? (2) What steps will you take to reach that goal? (3) Who from the community is needed to help plan your Help-a-thon? (4) What resources—such as equipment, money, or food—will be needed? Collect the charts, and post them around the room.

Reflection "How would your Help-a-thon positively influence our community? How does working together as a team strengthen community building?"

DAY 4 ▪ Healthy Community, Healthy You

Arrival Welcome

Greet each student by name as they enter.

Announcements

> Hello, Help-a-thoners!
>
> As you wrap up your planning, think about how you might inspire others to join your volunteer efforts.
>
> How might you promote your Help-a-thon? What is one highlight you could share with someone who is interested in helping? Be ready to share.

Point out today's (and/or this weekend's) key school and team events.

Acknowledgments

Maître d' Call out a table grouping (for example: "Table for 3!"). Students quickly form groups of that number. Ask open-ended questions for groups to discuss (see examples in margin). Remind students to say "hello" to every group member before they start each conversation, and remind them that each group member should share an idea. Repeat as time allows, continuing to vary the table size.

Maître d' Examples

➡ **Table for 2:** What are some questions interested volunteers might ask about your Help-a-thon?

➡ **Table for 3:** When could your Help-a-thon be scheduled? Consider the time needed for other school events and activities.

➡ **Table for 4:** Which adults from school could assist with your Help-a-thon, and how?

➡ **Table for 2:** How might you promote your Help-a-thon?

Activity

Help-a-thon Action Plan, Part 2 With their action plan group from yesterday, students create a poster, radio, or web advertisement to promote their Help-a-thon. Then they present their ads to the whole group, and later, to the school community on a school bulletin board, website, or public announcement system. During future Advisories, students could finalize their action plans and decide on next steps with you, such as presenting their action plans to the greater community (or a specific organization) for approval.

Reflection Gather everyone in a circle. Ask: "How did planning this project strengthen our Advisory community? How will implementing these Help-a-thons strengthen the greater community?"

Honoring Diversity

Understand others' perspectives and experience how diversity strengthens communities

---

Skills Practiced This Week

Active listening

Making personal connections

Building community

Drawing conclusions

Valuing diversity

DAY 1 ▪ Appreciating Differences

Arrival Welcome

Greet each student by name as they enter. Remind students to read the announcements message.

Announcements

> Welcome, Team!
>
> As we've learned throughout our Advisories together, we have many commonalities and also many things that make each of us unique. This week we're going to explore these differences and talk about how to appreciate diversity.
>
> On an index card, write 3 positive things that make you uniquely "you": (1) a family tradition; (2) a favorite activity or interest; (3) a skill or talent that you have. Be ready to share.

Include upcoming school and team events in your messages this week.

Acknowledgments

Info Exchange Students mix and mingle, greeting each other by name. On your signal, they stop, form pairs, and exchange cards without looking at them. (Consider participating in the exchange.) Do two more rounds of exchanges to ensure that all cards are anonymous. On your next signal, students form pairs and discuss what's on the cards they're holding and any personal connection to it. Finally, students exchange cards with their partner one last time and return to their table groups.

Activity

Analyzing Data Give each table group chart paper and assign a recorder. Tablemates share the information on their Info Exchange cards, and the recorder lists the ideas on their chart (for example: Japanese tea ceremony). Then each group member stars any ideas they connect to and highlights any ideas they would like to learn more about. Display everyone's charts. As a whole group, analyze the similarities and differences of the collected data. Students will reference the charts throughout this week's Advisory.

Reflection "How do you think our similarities and differences make us a stronger team?"

DAY 2 ▪ Alliance Unite

Arrival Welcome

Greet each student by name as they enter.

Announcements

Hi, Team!

Yesterday we learned about the many things that make each of us unique. Today we're going to further explore these differences.

Quote of the Day "Diversity: the art of thinking independently together." —MALCOLM FORBES, PUBLISHER, ENTREPRENEUR

Review the other groups' charts from yesterday. Star any of their ideas that you connect to, and circle any ideas you'd like to learn more about.

Point out today's key school and team events.

Acknowledgments

Around-the-Table Sharing Students greet their tablemates by name and take turns sharing one idea they circled that they'd like to learn more about. (Consider joining in on this activity.)

Activity

Interview Students pair up with someone from another table group and share one thing they listed on their index card from yesterday. Then students take turns asking their partner questions about what they shared. After a few minutes, students share one thing they learned about their partner with the whole group. (Consider pairing up with a student or joining a partnership to make a group of three.)

Reflection Gather everyone in a circle. Ask: "What did you learn about the members of our Advisory that you didn't know before? What does the Quote of the Day mean to you?"

Honoring Diversity

Understand others' perspectives and experience how diversity strengthens communities

Maître d' Examples

➤ **Table for 4:** "What are some types of discrimination?"

➤ **Table for 2:** "Why do you think some people discriminate?"

➤ **Table for 3:** "How can people help those who are discriminated against?"

➤ **Table for 4:** "How can we bring awareness about discrimination and promote acceptance and appreciation of people's differences?"

NOTE Refer to "Prepare students to handle serious news" on page 8 for tips on how to help students discuss serious news in a respectful manner.

DAY 3 ▪ What Is Discrimination?

Arrival Welcome

Greet each student by name as they enter. Encourage students to do a quick binder check as they get settled (see page 17).

Announcements

> Hello, Allies,
>
> Discrimination is the unjust treatment of a specific person because of race, gender, religion, socioeconomic status, or other factors. For example, at one time in America, women and people of color were not allowed to vote.
>
> Think about an instance of discrimination. It can be something you experienced, witnessed, read, or heard about. Be ready to share.

Point out today's key school and team events.

Acknowledgments

Maître d' Call out a table grouping (for example: "Table for 3!"). Students quickly form groups of that number and discuss their response to the announcements prompt. Then call out a new table grouping and ask a question relating to discrimination (see examples in margin). Repeat as time allows, continuing to vary the table size.

Activity

Love It or Leave It! Students stand or stay seated at their desks. Call out the title of a movie, TV show, book, or song, and then say "Love it or leave it?" Going in turn, students quickly throw their arms up in the air as they say "Love it" or stomp their feet as they say "Leave it," depending on whether they like or dislike what you called out. Repeat with a new topic as time allows.

Reflection "Think about the choices you could freely make during today's activities. How can discrimination affect people's choices?"

DAY 4 ■ Celebrating Diversity

Arrival Welcome

Greet each student by name as they enter. Consider adding in a handshake.

Announcements

> Hello, Team!
>
> Today you're going to use what you've learned about diversity to help promote appreciation of people's differences and celebrate diversity.
>
> **Quote of the Day** "Sticks in a bundle are unbreakable." —PROVERB
>
> Pick up an Appreciating Differences LSF Chart. List what you think appreciating differences should Look, Sound, and Feel like here at school.

Point out today's (and/or this weekend's) key school and team events.

Acknowledgments

Swap Meet Students mix and mingle, greeting each other with a handshake or a low five. On your signal, students find a partner and exchange ideas from their Appreciating Differences LSF Charts.* Encourage students to record any of their partner's ideas that they connect with. (Consider filling out and sharing your own chart.) Repeat for two to four more rounds. Collect everyone's charts.

Activity

Part One: Museum Walk Display the completed Appreciating Differences LSF Charts around the room. Have students walk around and review them. As they do, they draw a star next to any idea they connect with. (Consider starring ideas you connect with.)

Part Two: Celebrate Diversity Hand each student a sticky note and have them write down one way to celebrate diversity at school. (Consider sharing your own sticky note.) Post everyone's sticky notes, and invite volunteers to describe their idea.

Reflection Gather everyone in a circle. Ask: "Think about the ideas we posted. How might we put some of them into action?"

*An LSF Chart template is available to download; see page 19.

Upstanding Students

Devise and practice plans to prevent bullying in school to build a safer community

---

Skills Practiced This Week

Assertiveness
Building community
Empathy
Responsibility

Graffiti Headings

➡ How to respond if bullied

➡ How to respond if you witness bullying

➡ Whom to report bullying to

➡ How to report cyberbullying

➡ How to prevent future bullying

DAY 1 ▪ Be Brave

Arrival Welcome

Greet each student by name as they enter. Remind students to read the announcements message.

Announcements

Welcome, Brave Students!

Pacer's National Bullying Prevention Center reports that more than 1 out of every 5 students reports being bullied, and that 57% of bullying scenarios stop when a peer intervenes.

Quote of the Day "You must never be fearful about what you are doing when it is right." —ROSA PARKS, CIVIL RIGHTS ACTIVIST

What does it mean to be brave and stand up for your peers in school and on social media? Be ready to share.

Source for statistics: Pacer's National Bullying Prevention Center, www.pacer.org/bullying

Include upcoming school and team events in your messages this week.

Acknowledgments

Around-the-Table Sharing Students greet each of their tablemates by name, and take turns sharing their response to the announcements prompt. Ask a few volunteers to share their thoughts with the whole group.

Activity

Graffiti Post chart paper around the room with the headings shown at left. Students "graffiti" their ideas on the charts (starting at any chart, going in any order, writing in any style anywhere on the chart). Assign small groups to find common themes and trends among the ideas on the charts. Each group shares a summary of their findings with the whole group. Post the completed charts for reference this week.

Reflection "What is one action you could take this week to help prevent bullying?

DAY 2 ■ Get Up, Stand Up

Arrival Welcome

Greet each student by name as they enter. Consider adding in a handshake or a high five.

Announcements

Hello, Upstanders!

An upstander is someone who acts when they see something wrong.

On an index card, write down one idea for each of the following: (1) how to respond to bullying; (2) whom to report to if you experience or witness bullying; (3) how to prevent future bullying. (You can review yesterday's Graffiti charts for ideas.)

Point out today's key school and team events.

Acknowledgments

Info Exchange Students mix and mingle, greeting each other by name and giving high fives. On your signal, they stop, form pairs, and exchange index cards without looking at them. Do two more exchanges in this way to ensure that all cards are anonymous. On your next signal, students form pairs and discuss what's on the cards they're holding. Finally, students exchange cards with their partner one last time and return to their table groups.

Activity

Analyzing Data In their table group, students share the information on their Info Exchange cards. Then they determine their top three ideas (one idea from each announcements category). Each group reports the three ideas from their cards to the whole group. Label and post three pieces of chart paper, one for each category. Have each group write their top idea for each category on the corresponding chart paper. As a whole group, analyze the similarities of the collected data. Leave charts posted for the rest of the week.

Reflection "How does this data compare to the Graffiti charts from yesterday?"

Upstanding Students

Devise and practice plans to prevent bullying in school to build a safer community

---

Role-Play Guidelines

➤ You or another adult should always take the part of anyone exhibiting negative behaviors, such as a student bullying others. (Having students act out negative behaviors can backfire by reinforcing those negative behaviors.)

➤ Prompt observers to notice the specific, positive actions the actors demonstrate.

➤ Remind students to use respectful words and give positive feedback when debriefing.

DAY 3 ▪ Act Out

Arrival Welcome

Greet each student by name as they enter. Encourage students to do a quick binder check as they get settled.

Announcements

Hello, Team!

Today you're going to Act Out Against Bullying in our school.

Quote of the Day "Your positive actions combined with positive thinking results in success." —SHIV KHERA, AUTHOR, MOTIVATIONAL SPEAKER, ACTIVIST

Review our charts from yesterday. Star your number-one idea for each category. Be ready to share why you chose each one.

Point out today's key school and team events.

Acknowledgments

Group Brainstorm In their table group, students discuss their responses to the announcements prompt. Ask a few volunteers to share with the whole group why they chose one of their ideas.

Activity

Part 1: Tally Results As a whole group, tally the starred items on the charts. Circle the top choice for each category.

Part 2: "Act Out Against Bullying" Role-Play The goal of this role-play is to give students practice for how to respond to bullying (see guidelines in the margin). As a whole group, choose a situation based on the number-one idea for how to respond to bullying. Ask two or three students to serve as actors with you (or another adult), and together, privately plan your role-play. Have everyone else jot down their ideas about how they'd handle the situation. Perform the role-play (2–3 minutes), and then debrief as a whole group, focusing on positive strategies the students think worked. If time allows, role-play the same situation or a different one with a new group of students.

Reflection "How would you have responded to the situation? Share your ideas with a partner."

DAY 4 ▪ Stronger in Numbers

Arrival Welcome

Greet each student by name as they enter.

Announcements

> Hello, Stand-Up Students!
>
> **Quote of the Day** "Whenever one person stands up and says, 'Wait a minute, this is wrong,' it helps other people do the same."
> —GLORIA STEINEM, ACTIVIST, JOURNALIST
>
> Which adults in our school might you report to if you experience or witness bullying? Write down your answer on a piece of paper. Don't write your name on it. Then crumple it into a "snowball."

Point out today's (and/or this weekend's) key school and team events.

Acknowledgments

Snowball Students form a circle and gently toss their "snowball" into the center. Students pick up one snowball near them and share what's on the paper with the whole group. On a chart or whiteboard, write down students' ideas. Brainstorm additional ideas, including ways to anonymously report bullying.

Activity

Speak Up Anti-Bullying Campaign Students work in small groups to create collages, word splashes, or posters incorporating the information they learned this week. Each group must include at least one idea about (1) how to respond to bullying; (2) whom to report to; and (3) how to prevent future bullying. Have each group share their three ideas with the whole group. Collect the finished work, and post it on a school bulletin board for the greater school community.

Reflection "Looking back on this week, list three big ideas that will help you if you experience or witness bullying, two questions you have about bullying, and one takeaway or practical tip about bullying you plan to put into action."

ONE-DAY PLANS

One-Day Responsive Advisory Meeting Plans for Specific Occasions

Every school year has its ups and downs, and the unexpected can always happen. These one-day plans can be used to bolster the ups, cushion the downs, and address the unexpected.

At certain times throughout the year, students may need extra support or encouragement due to events or circumstances happening within or outside the school. For example, students might have mixed emotions on the day before a long vacation break, or a traumatic event such as a death in the community can result in feelings of grief, fear, or anger. Structuring a Responsive Advisory Meeting specifically for an atypical day can reaffirm the positive relationships students have with you and their Advisory peers and help them feel safe and supported in school.

The special one-day Responsive Advisory Meeting plans on the following pages are flexible and adaptable. You can use them to address the specific needs of your Advisory students for a wide variety of unexpected events, both positive and negative, as well as those times throughout the year when you know students will need a little extra support.

Here are some tips on how to use these one-day Responsive Advisory Meeting plans.

Modify for the Situation

These plans are like multipurpose tools, easily adaptable to fit the goals of your Advisory group or classroom. They can be made shorter or longer based on the time available, and simpler or more complex based on students' needs. Individual activities in each plan can be used throughout the day as icebreakers, transitions, brain breaks, or conclusions to a lesson.

Consider Developmental Needs

Not every student will respond to special situations in the same way. Likewise, their developmental age may be ahead of or behind their chronological age. Giving them the support they need may mean modifying the plan, modeling behaviors before you start an activity, or substituting in a familiar activity that will appeal to your students and give them the confidence to participate.

Encourage Participation

Students learn best when they're actively participating. The activities in these plans are meant to support all students in feeling valued, both as an individual and as a member of the Advisory group. Depending on the situation and the individual student, encourage some level of participation, such as being an active observer, serving as the note-taker or timekeeper, or engaging in a way that best suits their needs at that moment in time.

Reuse

While each plan is geared toward a specific type of event, each one can also be adapted for other situations. For instance, "Celebrations" (see page 197) could be used for a major achievement, such as the completion of a big research paper, or for a milestone task, such as completing a difficult step in an experiment. Reusing a plan can also help students become more adept with the skills required for success, and it provides a comforting familiarity that can lead to more authentic student engagement.

Work in Current Content

Responsive Advisory Meeting is always an opportunity to bring current areas of study into the classroom. Extra practice can boost students' skills and build their confidence. Reviewing academic content using the collaborative foundation of Responsive Advisory Meeting activities can also make the concepts more approachable for students.

Keep Routines Consistent

Regardless of circumstance, the routine of Responsive Advisory Meeting offers a safe space in times of uncertainty. Knowing what to expect and having an adult check in with them regularly helps reassure students that they are part of a caring, supportive community.

Have Fun!

Students associate Responsive Advisory Meeting with positive, engaging activities, and for this reason, they usually look forward to participating. Students who are invested in what they're doing are more motivated, focused, and engaged, and more likely to support one another and make the most of their Advisory time together.

Peer Pressure Role-Play

Arrival Welcome

Greet each student by name as they enter. Remind them to read the announcements message.

Announcements

Hi, Team!

Consider this situation: James is sitting with Amir at a schoolwide assembly. James tells Tina that she should sit on the other side of the room because she doesn't "look as cool" as the other students sitting with them.

What advice would you give Tina? Amir? James? Be ready to share your ideas.

Include upcoming school and team events in your message.

Acknowledgments

What's Your Advice? One student in each table group begins by greeting the student to their left: "Good morning, _____. What's your advice for Tina?" The student returns the greeting and shares their advice. Continue around the table so everyone can suggest advice first for Tina, then for Amir, and then for James. Invite a few students to summarize their table group's ideas for the whole group.

Activity

Communication Role-Play Assign or let students volunteer for the four parts: Gabriel, Gabriel's inner thoughts, Anthony, and Anthony's inner thoughts. Hand out Communication Role-Play* scripts. Explain the goal for the observers: to consider why Anthony and Gabriel's spoken words are different from what they're thinking, and to brainstorm advice for their situation. If time allows, have the whole group brainstorm answers to these questions: What would you do if you were Gabriel? If you were Anthony? Then brainstorm an ending to the scene.

Reflection Gather everyone in a circle. Ask: "How would this situation be different if Anthony and Gabriel said what was on their minds (in respectful ways)?"

*A Communication Role-Play script is available to download; see page 19.

TIPS

→ Teach and model appropriate audience behavior before you get started, as needed.

→ Plan how to describe the dilemma and the goal. For example: "Today you're going to see friends navigate a difficult situation. Neither is saying what they are really thinking. Your goal is to think about advice you would give them."

→ Think ahead about who would take each role seriously, but be sure that over the course of the year every student has a chance to participate in a role-play.

→ Give performers an opportunity to practice in advance and in private. Even a few minutes of practice can make for a more productive role-play.

After a Long Break

Arrival Welcome

Greet each student by name as they enter. Remind them to read the announcements message. Have a few longer exchanges to get a sense of the group's mood about returning to school.

Announcements

Welcome Back, Team!

I hope you all had a nice break.

Quote of the Day "Every new day, we must refocus, to see the beauty of the moment." —LAILAH GIFTY AKITA, AUTHOR AND FOUNDER OF SMART YOUTH VOLUNTEERS FOUNDATION

What's one thing you do that helps you get back (or stay) on track? Be ready to share.

Include upcoming school and team events in your message.

Acknowledgments

Mix and Mingle Students walk around the room, greeting each other by name and offering a handshake or other friendly gesture. Then they exchange responses to the announcements prompt. After students have talked with three to four classmates, ask a few to share one refocusing idea with the whole group. List these on chart paper or the whiteboard.

Activity

Switch Students put their right hand out in front of them, with the thumb up and all the fingers curled in, and put their left hand out with their index finger out and the thumb and other fingers curled in. When you call "Switch!" everyone switches the position of the index fingers and thumbs, so that the right hand now has the index finger pointing out and the left hand has the thumb up. Continue calling "Switch!" and alternating fingers and thumbs, starting out slowly and speeding up as you go along.

Reflection Gather everyone in a circle. Ask: "What's one thing you're looking forward to this week, and why?"

TIPS

➡ Students might struggle to get back into a school routine. Adjust activities as necessary to help them succeed. For example, instead of using Mix and Mingle, you could have students share ideas in table groups.

➡ Some students may forget to follow behavior expectations after being away from school for a number of days. Specific reminders and reinforcing language will help students stay on track. The list you create during acknowledgments is a good resource to refer them to.

Whole-Team Meeting

Arrival Welcome

Greet students by name as they enter the room. Remind them to read the announcements message.

Announcements

> Hi, Team!
>
> **Quote of the Day** "I know there is strength in the differences between us." —ANI DIFRANCO, SINGER-SONGWRITER, POET
>
> Think of one skill you recently learned or a favorite activity, class, book, etc. Write your response down anonymously on an index card and hand it to me. You'll then count off to form groups. We'll be using these cards during our whole-team meeting.

Include the agenda for the whole-team meeting in your message so students know what to expect. Display this message in your Advisory room and during the whole-team meeting.

Acknowledgments

What's the News? Students gather into groups according to their number. Each advisor joins a group. In their group, students and advisors greet each other with "Good morning, _____! What's the news?" Then going around the group, each person shares a positive recent event from their personal life, such as a book they're enjoying, a fun trip they took, or a relative who's visiting.

Activity

Just Like Me Explain that you'll be reading aloud a few students' and advisors' cards. As you read each prompt, students who feel it applies to them stand up (or raise hands if standing is difficult) and say "Just like me" at the same time. Start with your own example: "I like to watch TV mysteries." Read as many cards as time allows. Let students know you'll read the others at another Advisory meeting.

Reflection Gather students in a circle. Ask: "How does meeting as a whole team help strengthen our community?" Ask a few volunteers to share ideas with the whole group.

TIPS

- ➜ To make the most of this whole-team meeting, have all advisors participate in all four components. This will help students get to know and be known by all advisees on the team.

- ➜ Consider the logistics needed to fit all your team's Advisory groups safely into the same space in an orderly way.

- ➜ Model routines, such as entering the shared space, and be clear about expectations that enable a larger group to succeed together, especially listening and following directions.

- ➜ For the acknowledgments, consider having students sit with members of their own Advisory group as well as other Advisory groups, which might help certain students feel safer in a large group setting.

What's the Outcome?

Arrival Welcome

Greet each student by name as they enter. Remind them to read the announcements message.

Announcements

Hi, Advisory Team!

Quote of the Day "The true test of character is measured by how well a person makes decisions during difficult times." —JACK GANTOS, AUTHOR, NEWBERY MEDAL WINNER

When was the last time you made a difficult choice? How do you feel about it now? Be ready to share with your table group.

Include upcoming school and team events in your message.

Acknowledgments

Table Talk Students greet their tablemates and then take turns sharing their response to the announcements prompt. After all students have shared with their table group, ask for a few volunteers to share with the whole group.

Activity

What's the Outcome? Pass out What's the Outcome?* handouts. Explain that each student should choose the options they think are best and be ready to discuss why they made those decisions. Let students know that it will be their task to write an ending for each adventure. With a partner, they discuss their endings. Then ask the whole group: "What were the most difficult decisions to make? Did any ideas surprise you? How did your adventure end?" Seek out differing opinions, and encourage thoughtful discussions based on sound reasons and evidence. Encourage as many students to respond as time allows.

Reflection "If you were to create your own What's the Outcome scenario, what would the topic be, and why?"

*A What's the Outcome? template is available to download; see page 19.

Before a Long Break

Arrival Welcome

Greet each student by name as they enter. Remind them to read the announcements message.

Announcements

Hello, Advisory Team!

Quote of the Day "The ant is knowing and wise, but he doesn't know enough to take a vacation." —CLARENCE DAY, AUTHOR, CARTOONIST

Think about the goals you set for yourself earlier this year. How can vacations help us reach them? Be ready to share your ideas.

Include upcoming school and team events that occur during or right after the break in your message.

Acknowledgments

Inside-Outside Circles Students count off by twos. Ones form an inner circle and face out; twos form an outer circle and face in to form pairs. Partners greet each other by name and share their responses to the announcements prompt. Then twos move one person to their right, and greet and share responses with their new partner. Repeat for a few more rounds. If time allows, have volunteers share one idea with the whole group.

Activity

Do What I Said, Not What I Say Everyone stands at their desks. Call out an action (see directions at left). Students must follow the previously given action, not the current one. Play as many rounds as time allows, and increase the difficulty in each round by speeding up and adding new movements.

Reflection Gather everyone in a circle. Ask: "What are you most looking forward to during vacation? How might Clarence Day's quote apply to your vacation?"

Do What I Said, Not What I Say Directions

"Stand on one foot."
(students do nothing)

"Hop on one foot."
(students stand on one foot)

"Flap your arms."
(students hop on one foot)

"Pat your head."
(students flap their arms)

"Sit down."
(students pat their heads)

"Fold your hands on your desks."
(students sit down)

"Fold your hands on your desks."
(students fold their hands on their desks)

Celebrations

Arrival Welcome

Greet each student by name as they enter. Remind them to read the announcements message. Consider also giving a festive fist bump (for example, a fist bump followed by both student and teacher mimicking fireworks with their hands).

Announcements

Hey, Triumphant Team!

You did it! Give yourself a pat on the back for all you've accomplished. A task completed is an opportunity to reflect on what you've achieved—and a time to celebrate!

Think about a time when you celebrated an accomplishment. Why was it important to you to celebrate this event? Be ready to share.

Include upcoming school and team celebratory events, such as an awards ceremony, in your message.

Acknowledgments

Swap Meet Students mix and mingle, greeting each other with a handshake or low five. On your signal, students find a partner and exchange ideas in response to the announcements prompt. Repeat for three or four more rounds.

Activity

Put It to a Vote Have students vote on which of three activities they'd like to celebrate with—for example: Zoom (page 77), Body Drumming (page 161), or Elevens (page 65). If the vote is close, you can schedule the second choice activity for the next day.

Reflection Gather everyone in a circle. Say: "Take a moment to reflect on all who helped you achieve your goal. Name one person and how they helped you."

TIPS

➡ The type of achievement you are celebrating may impact the way you use this plan. For example, you can write more specifically about your group's accomplishments in the announcements message.

➡ Replace any of the activity options with activities that students have most enjoyed thus far this year.

➡ A celebration should be fun, but some students might take it as an opportunity to get silly or forget to follow behavior expectations. Specific reminders and reinforcing language can help these students stay on track.

Traumatic Events

TIPS

TIPS

➤ Each traumatic circumstance is unique. Consider who is most impacted by the situation, and alter the activities accordingly.

➤ Students who are silent may be having a harder time expressing themselves. Consider talking to those students one-on-one.

➤ Teach and model, as needed, to show students some appropriate ways to support their classmates.

Maître d' Examples

➤ **Table for 3:** What is one thing we can do to take care of each other today?

➤ **Table for 2:** What is one thing we can do to take care of each other the rest of this week?

➤ **Table for 4:** How can you support classmates who need to talk?

➤ **Table for 3:** Is there something on your mind right now that you'd like to share with your table?

Arrival Welcome

Greet each student by name as they enter. Remind them to read the announcements message. Consider offering a warm smile, a hand on their shoulder, or other reassuring gesture.

Announcements

Dear Advisory Community,

Today is a difficult day for all of us. This is a safe place to express your feelings and support others as they express theirs.

Quote of the Day "Give sorrow words." —WILLIAM SHAKESPEARE, PLAYWRIGHT

Think of one or two people you feel most comfortable talking to when you are upset.

Make it clear during announcements that you will be available for anyone who needs to talk.

Acknowledgments

Around-the-Table Chat Students greet each of their tablemates by name and take turns sharing their response to the announcements prompt. Then they have a more free-flowing conversation about what the people they named have in common.

Activity

Maître d' Call out a table grouping (for example: "Table for 3!"). Students form standing groups of that number to discuss their response to a question you pose (see examples in margin). Repeat as time allows, continuing to vary the table size. Join in on discussions, and remind and redirect any students who may be struggling.

Reflection Gather everyone in a circle and discuss why it's important to "give sorrow words." End Advisory with a group check-in. Let students share any worries and concerns. If a lot of students want to share, let them know when you're available to talk and that the conversation can continue during the next Advisory meeting.

Friendship Calculator

TIPS

- Replace the example in today's announcements with one that is specific to you as a friend. This is an opportunity for your Advisory group to get to know you better and continue strengthening the bonds of the Advisory group community.

- Make it clear that students will keep people's names anonymous when evaluating specific friendships.

- Encourage students to reflect on their scores. For example, if a student scored a 3 for "accept apologies when feelings get hurt," ask them to think of a time when they refused to accept an apology and how it could have gone differently. Or, if a student scored a 1 for "honest and loyal" ask them to think about specific times they've shown loyalty to friends.

Arrival Welcome

Greet each student by name as they enter. Remind them to read the announcements message. Consider giving a behind-the-back low five.

Announcements

Dear Team,

One of my favorite cartoon friendships is Calvin and Hobbes because they're so comfortable being themselves around each other and always look out for each other, even when they argue.

Think of a friendship from a book, movie, or TV show that you admire, and two reasons why.

Include upcoming school and team events in your message.

Acknowledgments

Friendship Calculator Have each student complete the Friendship Calculator* handout. Explain that the goal is for each student to answer the questions as honestly as possible about one of their friendships. Once everyone is done, hand out the score chart. Give students time to calculate and consider their scores. Then with their table partner, students share something that surprised them about their score.

Activity

Mix and Mingle Students walk around the room, greeting each other by name and offering a handshake or some other friendly gesture. Then they share their response to the announcements prompt. After greeting at least four classmates, they return to their table group. Going around the room, students share one common quality of the friendships people mentioned with the whole group. List these on chart paper and post on the wall where everyone can see.

Reflection "Looking at the qualities listed on the wall, which one do you think is most important to have? What actions might you take to strengthen your friendships with others?"

*A Friendship Calculator template is available to download; see page 19.

FIVE-MINUTE PLANS

Five-Minute Responsive Advisory Meeting Plans

A core strength of Responsive Advisory Meeting is its flexibility—elements can be used as classroom entry or closing routines, or seamlessly integrated into lesson plans.

Sometimes it's just not possible to fit a full-length Responsive Advisory Meeting into the daily schedule. Special events, testing schedules, a whole-school assembly, and early dismissal days can reduce or eliminate the time usually reserved for Advisory. Fortunately, Responsive Advisory Meeting can be incorporated into any academic lesson plan without sacrificing the rich social-emotional learning and community building that it provides.

This section offers mini-plans that can be adapted for any content area. These plans allow you to move through all four Responsive Advisory Meeting components in five minutes or less. The plans are intended to serve as models that can easily be adapted to your current unit of study, so you can build off of what is currently being taught in that subject on any given day. They are best used at the beginning of a class period to help students quickly connect as a learning community and introduce them to the academic goal.

Bringing Responsive Advisory Meeting into the classroom on even the busiest days helps you maintain a positive relationship with students, contributes to consistency in students' routines, and encourages the social-emotional growth that supports rigorous learning.

Here are a few tips on how to use these mini-plans.

Connect to Current Content

Use these mini-plans to complement current units of study—for example, to pre-view or introduce new content, give extra practice with a skill, or review previous learning. The sample messages and corresponding activities are easy to tailor to your specific lesson plans. Use the tips in the side column next to each mini-plan for extra guidance.

Use in Any Class

These plans are useful even on days when there is enough time for regular Advisory groups to meet. The plans can be used to start any class or to transition into a new subject area. Components from each plan can also be used as introductions, ice-breakers, or brain breaks. For example, you might use the arrival welcome, announce-ments, and acknowledgments to start the class period and then use the activity to end it.

Prepare Students

For students who are used to longer Responsive Advisory Meetings, let them know that you're using the same structure, just in a shorter time frame because of the change in their usual schedule. Remind students of the expectations for keeping discussions brief. You may also want to have students respond to a question or prompt as home-work the night before and then share their responses in class.

Expand When Possible

These mini-plans are meant to be compact, but they also contain the foundation for a full-length Responsive Advisory Meeting. You can use or adapt these mini-plans for your usual Advisory group meeting by expanding the acknowledgments and activity components and adding a reflection question at the end.

Making Connections

TIPS

➡ For the announcements prompt, you may want to note an example from your own life.

➡ Making personal connections is a great way for students to interact meaningfully with content. For example, students could brainstorm when they might use fractions in their everyday lives, visualize themselves in an important historical period, or consider the ways they impact their local ecosystem.

Arrival Welcome

Greet students by name with "Hola," "Bonjour," or a greeting in another language. Remind them to read the announcements message.

Announcements (2 minutes)

> Welcome, Writers,
>
> Last week, you read examples of personal narratives. This week, you're going to write your own.
>
> Think about one event in your life you might want to include in your personal narrative, and why.

Include assignments and news for the day.

Acknowledgments (2 minutes)

In their table group, students greet each other and take turns briefly sharing their life event and why they chose it.

Activity (1 minute)

Just Like Me Have a volunteer from each group call out their life event idea. All students who also had that idea (or one very similar to it) stand up (or raise hands if standing is difficult) and say "Just like me!" Do as many rounds as time allows.

Exploring a Concept

TIPS

➥ This lesson can be adapted to fit any unit of study.

➥ The announcements prompt is designed to stimulate thinking, so it can be as broad as "What is one thing you know about industrialization?" or "When have you used chemistry outside of school?"

➥ This mini-plan can also be connected to topics like analyzing different perspectives in literature, making predictions in science, or learning about governmental checks and balances in social studies.

Arrival Welcome

Greet each student by name as they enter. Remind them to read the announcements message.

Announcements (1 minute)

Welcome, Mathematicians,

Today our focus is on probability. What do you think are the chances we'll study probability tomorrow? Write your answer here:

Think about what you'd like to learn about probability, and why.

Include assignments and news for the day.

Acknowledgments (2 minutes)

In their table group, students take turns sharing one sentence about what they hope to learn about probability, and why.

Activity (2 minutes)

Elevens In small groups, students stand with one hand behind their backs and say in unison: "One, two, three—eleven!" On "eleven," they silently throw their hands into the center of their group as they flash any number of fingers—from zero (a fist) to five—to try to total eleven fingers. If the total number of fingers does not equal eleven, they try again. If they equal eleven, they join another group and continue playing until time is up.

Introducing a New Unit

Arrival Welcome

Greet students by name with a "Happy Wednesday" or similar greeting. Remind them to read the announcements message.

Announcements (1 minute)

Welcome, Artists [Musicians, Athletes],

Today we embark on a brand-new unit, pastels [major and minor scales, volleyball].

Think of one or more things you are most looking forward to learning about during this new unit.

Include assignments and news for the day.

Acknowledgments (2 minutes)

In their table group, students share one idea in response to the announcements prompt. If there's time, call on a few volunteers to share with the whole group.

Activity (2 minutes)

Love It or Leave It! (variation) Name a topic related to a previous unit of study, such as practicing free throws, drawing with charcoal, or sight reading. First say "Love it?" Students with that response throw their hands in the air and say "Love it!" Then say "Leave it?" Students with that response stomp their feet and say "Leave it!" Repeat with new topics as time allows.

Practicing Observation Skills

Arrival Welcome

Greet students by name with a high five as they enter. Remind them to read the announcements message.

Announcements (1 minute)

> Welcome, Scientists,
>
> Yesterday you started your experiments. Today you will continue to observe the reactions and collect more data.
>
> Think about your most important observation from yesterday.

Include assignments and news for the day.

Acknowledgments (2 minutes)

At table groups, students take turns briefly sharing their most important observation.

Activity (2 minutes)

Sound Check Have students gather in a circle and close their eyes. Explain that they're going to be completely silent for 15 seconds, and that they should listen and focus on whatever sound they become most aware of (such as a fan or footsteps in the hallway). Signal to begin the silence. At your next signal they open their eyes, and quickly going around the circle, say which sound most stood out to them in the silence.

Pros and Cons

TIPS

➡ This sample lesson is focused on civics, which can be replaced with almost any unit of study without having to change the plan format significantly. Find a fact or concept in your current unit that lends itself to considering pros and cons, such as the decision a literary character makes, a math problem that can be solved multiple ways, or a difficult choice a historical figure must face.

➡ If you have extra time, consider holding a mini-debate during acknowledgments with one group taking the "pro" side and the other the "con" side.

Arrival Welcome

Greet each student by name as they enter. Remind them to read the announcements message. Consider assigning each student a pro or con topic as they enter (for example, "homework—pro" or "pet goldfish—con") and asking the student to quickly respond with a corresponding pro or con.

Announcements (2 minutes)

Welcome, Civic Leaders,

Yesterday you read an article about the plan to turn the old shoe factory into condos.

Think of one benefit (pro) and one drawback (con) to this plan.

Include assignments and news for the day.

Acknowledgments (2 minutes)

In their table group, students take turns sharing their one pro and one con.

Activity (1 minute)

Snap Wink On your signal, everyone winks their left eye and snaps with their right hand. When you call out "Switch," everyone winks their right eye and snaps with their left hand. Repeat, increasing the speed each time.

Further Resources

All the practices recommended in this book come from or are consistent with the *Responsive Classroom* approach to teaching—an evidence-based education approach associated with greater teacher effectiveness, higher student achievement, and improved school climate. *Responsive Classroom* practices help educators build competencies in four interrelated domains: engaging academics, positive community, effective management, and developmentally responsive teaching.

To learn more, see the following resources published by Center for Responsive Schools and available from www.responsiveclassroom.org • 800-360-6332.

The Power of Our Words for Middle School: Teacher Language That Helps Students Learn (from *Responsive Classroom*, 2016). Practical information, tips, and examples for improving the professional language you use with students. Through your use of words and tone, you can more fully engage students in their learning and support positive development in all areas of their lives.

Middle School Motivators: 22 Interactive Learning Structures (from *Responsive Classroom*, 2016). These easy-to-use structures encourage all students to give their best effort, focus on learning goals, and collaborate effectively with one another in dynamic, purposeful, and respectful ways.

Refocus and Recharge: 50 Brain Breaks for Middle Schoolers (from *Responsive Classroom*, 2016). Quick, easy-to-learn activities that give students much-needed mental and physical breaks from rigorous learning, and increase their ability to stay on task and focus on the content you teach.

Yardsticks: Child and Adolescent Development Ages 4–14, 4th edition (by Chip Wood, 2018). This accessible reference concisely charts children's development, shows what behavior you can expect to see in the classroom (and at home) at different ages, and outlines ways you can support students' social-emotional and academic learning and growth.

Yardsticks Guide Series: Common Developmental Characteristics in the Classroom and at Home, Grades K–8 (2018; based on *Yardsticks* by Chip Wood). Common characteristics of children's development are summarized in easy-to-scan, grade-specific guides for educators and parents.

Publisher's Acknowledgments

More than thirty years in the making, the *Responsive Classroom* approach to teaching continues to evolve thanks to the thousands of educators whose hard work and dedication continue to improve students' lives here and around the world. Over these years, we've published a wide variety of titles and developed numerous other resources to better support schools and teachers in four critical domains of education: engaging academics, positive community, effective classroom management, and developmentally responsive teaching. You can see a list of our books and other resources for middle school educators on page 209 and by visiting www.responsiveclassroom.org.

Because Advisory is such a core element of effective middle schools, Center for Responsive Schools committed its staff and resources to developing this book. Our hope is that the use of these Responsive Advisory Meeting plans will enhance the daily lives of middle school students and teachers, help them build stronger relationships with one another and throughout their schools and community, and contribute to lifelong wellness and success for every student.

Center for Responsive Schools wishes to thank the following middle school educators for their careful reading of and feedback on the manuscript:

Christine Diaz (7th–8th grades), Willis Junior High School, Chandler, Arizona

Brianna Rivers (6th–8th grades), Alfred G. Zanetti Montessori Magnet School, Springfield, Massachusetts

Joe Tilley (5th–6th grades), Metro Nashville Public Schools, Nashville, Tennessee

Special thanks go to the schools, especially to their teachers and students, that participated in the 2016 research study on Responsive Advisory Meeting done by the Center for Responsive Schools in partnership with Analytica, Inc. The time and effort they devoted to this research and the valuable feedback and insights they gave us have greatly shaped this book. We hope that as this book is read and used during Advisories, their efforts positively influence middle school students and teachers around the world.

About the Contributors

Michelle Benson is a full-time professional development designer and consultant for Center for Responsive Schools (CRS), working with teachers and school districts throughout the United States and the international school community. Michelle began her education career as a middle school English/Language Arts teacher. Prior to joining CRS, Michelle served as a secondary curriculum specialist for eight years in a rural school district in North Carolina.

Rio Clemente has been a sixth grade social studies teacher at Randolph Middle School in New Jersey since 2001. In 2004, he founded the Random Acts of Kindness club, which inspires students to perform acts of kindness for each other, the school, and the greater community. He has been practicing the *Responsive Classroom* approach since 2014 and has been a *Responsive Classroom* consulting teacher since 2016.

Nicole Doner was a fifth grade teacher in both Burlington and Essex, Vermont, where she practiced the *Responsive Classroom* approach for over fifteen years. Currently, Nicole is a full-time educational consultant and coach for Center for Responsive Schools.

Jeannie Holenko is a sixth grade teacher at Oak Bluffs School in Oak Bluffs, Massachusetts. She has been creating safe, joyful, and engaging classrooms using the *Responsive Classroom* approach for more than twenty years, and has been a *Responsive Classroom* consulting teacher for the past thirteen years.

Dana Januszka began her teaching career in South Brunswick, New Jersey. She has been practicing and teaching the *Responsive Classroom* approach for over eighteen years, most recently working on the research and development team for the middle school approach. Currently, Dana is coaching educators and school leaders in building inclusive and optimal learning environments.

Amber Searles had practiced and taught the *Responsive Classroom* approach for middle school for four years before becoming a program developer for Center for Responsive Schools, where she focuses on creating *Responsive Classroom* middle school content. Before working for CRS, she taught sixth through eighth grades at Brewer Middle School in Greenwood, South Carolina.

About the Publisher

Center for Responsive Schools, Inc., a not-for-profit educational organization, is the developer of *Responsive Classroom*®, an evidence-based education approach associated with greater teacher effectiveness, higher student achievement, and improved school climate. *Responsive Classroom* practices help educators build competencies in four interrelated domains: engaging academics, positive community, effective management, and developmentally responsive teaching. We offer the following resources for educators:

PROFESSIONAL DEVELOPMENT SERVICES

➧ Workshops for K–8 educators (locations around the country and internationally)

➧ On-site consulting services to support implementation

➧ Resources for site-based study

➧ Annual conferences for K–8 educators

PUBLICATIONS AND RESOURCES

➧ Books on a wide variety of *Responsive Classroom* topics

➧ Free monthly newsletter

➧ Extensive library of free articles on our website

FOR DETAILS, CONTACT:

Responsive Classroom®

Center for Responsive Schools, Inc.
85 Avenue A, P.O. Box 718
Turners Falls, Massachusetts 01376-0718

800-360-6332 www.responsiveclassroom.org
info@responsiveclassroom.org